Science
made easy

Key Stage 2
Ages 10–11

Authors Mike Evans, Linda Ellis,
Hugh Westrup and David Evans
Consultants David Evans and Kara Pranikoff

Certificate ☆ ☆ ☆ ★

Congratulations to ....
(write your name here)
for successfully finishing this book.

☆ *You're a star!* ☆

DK

What kind of animal is this?

Science facts

There are many different species of animal. Scientists use keys to identify them. Being able to use keys is an important skill. To find the name of an animal, you can use a branching key. Start at the top of the key and answer **Yes** or **No** to each question. Follow the branches until you reach the end.

Science quiz

Arthropods are small animals with jointed legs. The word **arthropod** means "jointed legs".

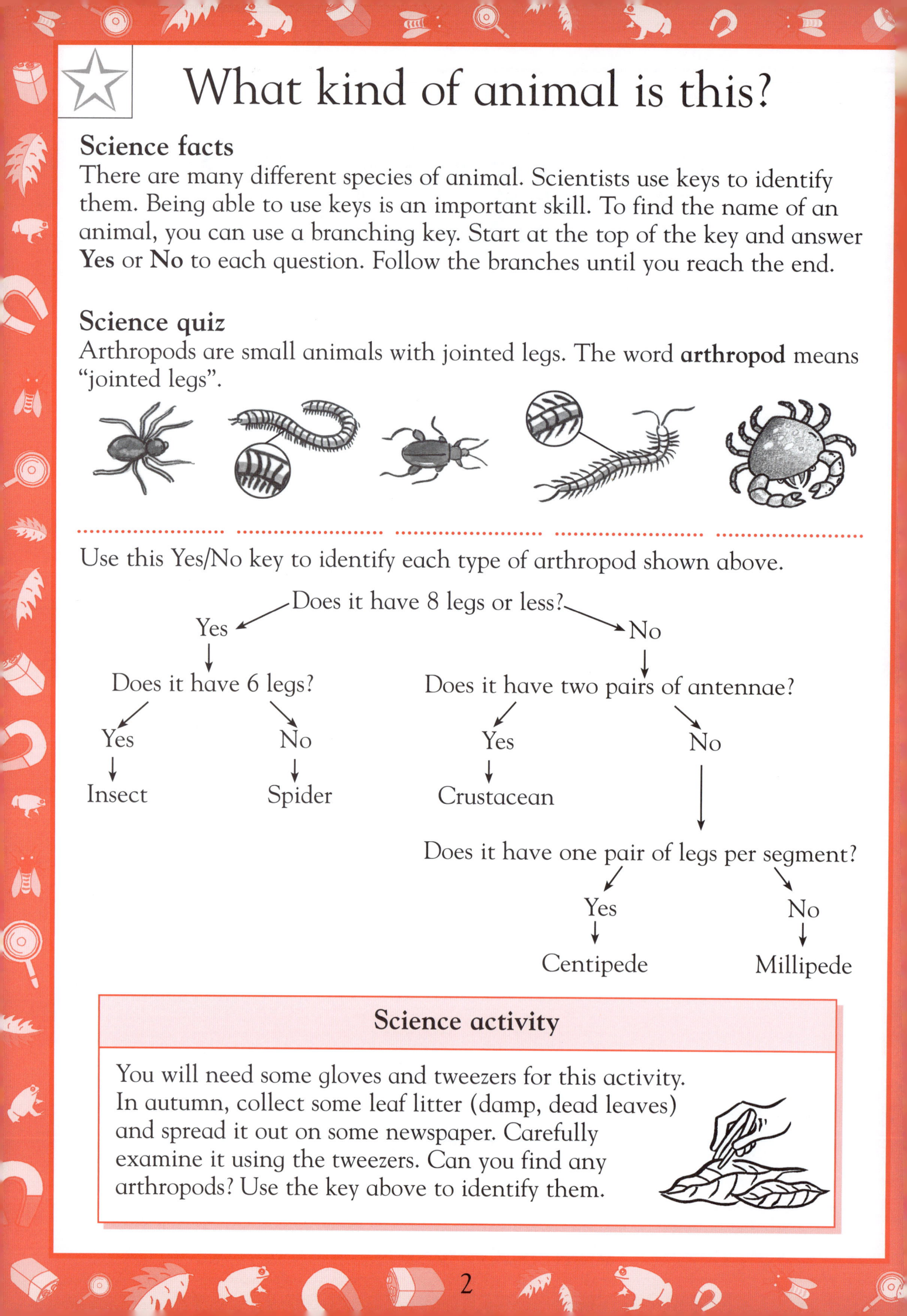

Use this Yes/No key to identify each type of arthropod shown above.

Does it have 8 legs or less?

Yes → Does it have 6 legs?

Yes → Insect

No → Spider

No → Does it have two pairs of antennae?

Yes → Crustacean

No → Does it have one pair of legs per segment?

Yes → Centipede

No → Millipede

Science activity

You will need some gloves and tweezers for this activity. In autumn, collect some leaf litter (damp, dead leaves) and spread it out on some newspaper. Carefully examine it using the tweezers. Can you find any arthropods? Use the key above to identify them.

What sort of plant is this?

Science facts

Trees are plants. There are many different types, or species, of tree. Based on observable characteristics, branching keys can be used to identify different species.

Science quiz

Look at the pictures of the four twigs below. Use the key to identify each one. Write your answers on the dotted lines.

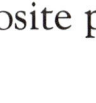
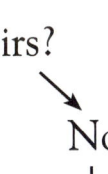

....

....

....

....

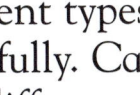

Do the buds grow in opposite pairs?

Yes — No

Are the buds black, small and pointed? — Are the buds long and thin?

Yes — No — Yes — No

Ash — Horse chestnut — Beech — Oak

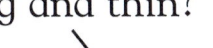

Science activity

In spring, collect different types of twig. Examine the buds carefully. Can you make a key to help identify different species?

Can you make a bird key?

Science facts

Branching keys work best when things are divided into groups and then further divided into smaller groups. When putting birds into groups, you could first divide them into wading birds (those with webbed feet) and non-wading birds and then think of some subsets, such as size, shape or colour of beak.

Science quiz

Swan

Blackbird

Duck

Moorhen

Magpie

Make a branching key for the birds above using their different characteristics.

Science activity

Birds that often visit gardens and parks include the thrush, starling, sparrow, blue tit, robin, wren, crow and rook. Leave some scraps of bread or nuts on the ground in your garden or local park. Which birds come to eat them? Make a key for these birds.

Can you make a plant key?

Science facts

Yes/No keys can also be written as numbered questions. Answer the questions below to identify the three plants in the pictures.

1. Is the plant over 2 metres tall?
   If yes, go to 2; if no, go to 3.
2. It is an oak tree.
3. Does the plant have a flower?
   If yes, go to 4; if no, go to 5.
4. It is a daffodil.
5. It is moss.

Science quiz

Make a Yes/No key to distinguish between the different flowers shown below.

Iris

Rose

Daffodil

....
....
....
....
....
....
....
....
....

Science activity

Look at some plants in your garden or local park. Can you make a Yes/No key to identify them? Ask some friends to try your key. Does it work?

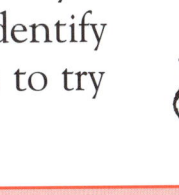

How do microbes help?

Science facts

Microbes, or micro-organisms, are living things that are often too small to be seen. Three common types of microbes are bacteria, viruses and some fungi. These organisms need food, warmth and moisture to grow and reproduce. Some microbes feed on things that were once living, such as fallen leaves and dead animals, causing them to break down, or decay. The decayed materials mix with the soil, providing essential nutrients for plants to use. Without this process, the nutrients in the soil would run out. Microbes also help us make some of our foods, such as bread, cheese, yogurt, beer and wine. They feed on the sugar in grain, fruit or milk, giving these foods a special texture and taste.

Science quiz

Zarine put the following items into a large polythene bag. She took them out again after two weeks. In the boxes below, write **D** for the items that would have decayed and **U** for those that would be unchanged.

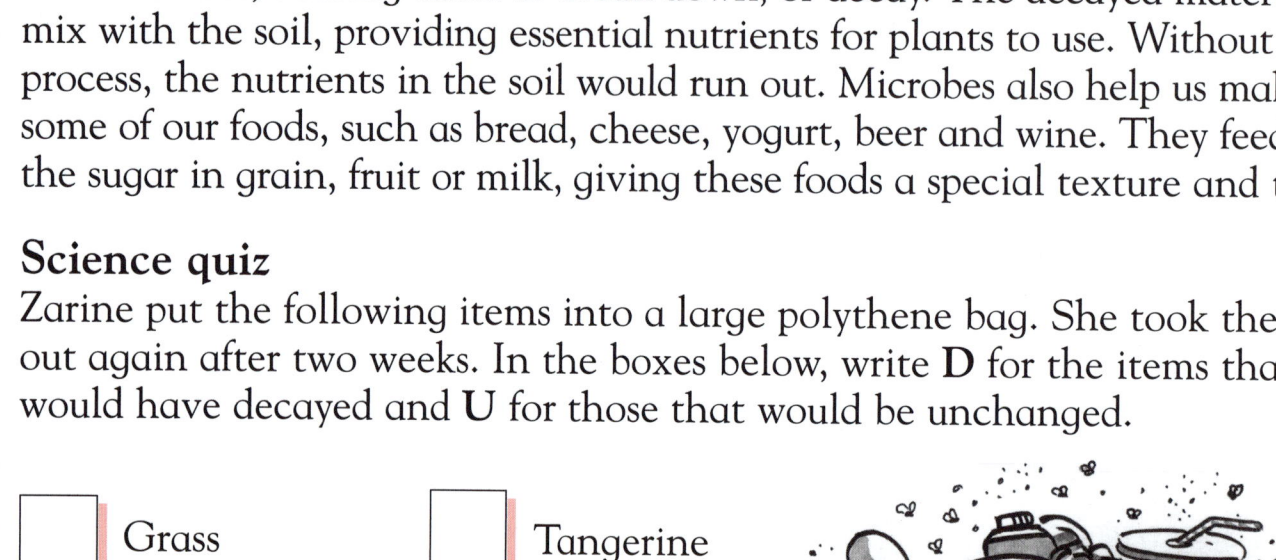

	Grass		Tangerine
	Plastic spoon		Bread
	Apple peel		Leaves
	Cola can		Nylon tights

Why have some of the items not decayed?

....

....

Science activity

To grow microbes, mix one teaspoon of dried yeast and half a teaspoon of sugar in half a cup of slightly warm water. Add enough of this mixture to 125 grams of flour to make the grains stick together. Make a ball from the dough and place it on a plate in a warm place. What happens?

How are microbes harmful?

Science facts

Some microbes, often called germs, can cause illness or disease. Chickenpox, mumps and measles are caused by microbes. They are infectious diseases. Some microbes can cause food to decay. Mouldy bread or fruit, rotten meat and sour milk are examples of decayed food. If eaten, this rotten food and drink can cause stomach upsets. Other microbes cause tooth decay. You can protect yourself from harmful microbes by storing and preparing food properly, cleaning your teeth, washing your hands and by not coming in close contact with ill people.

Science quiz

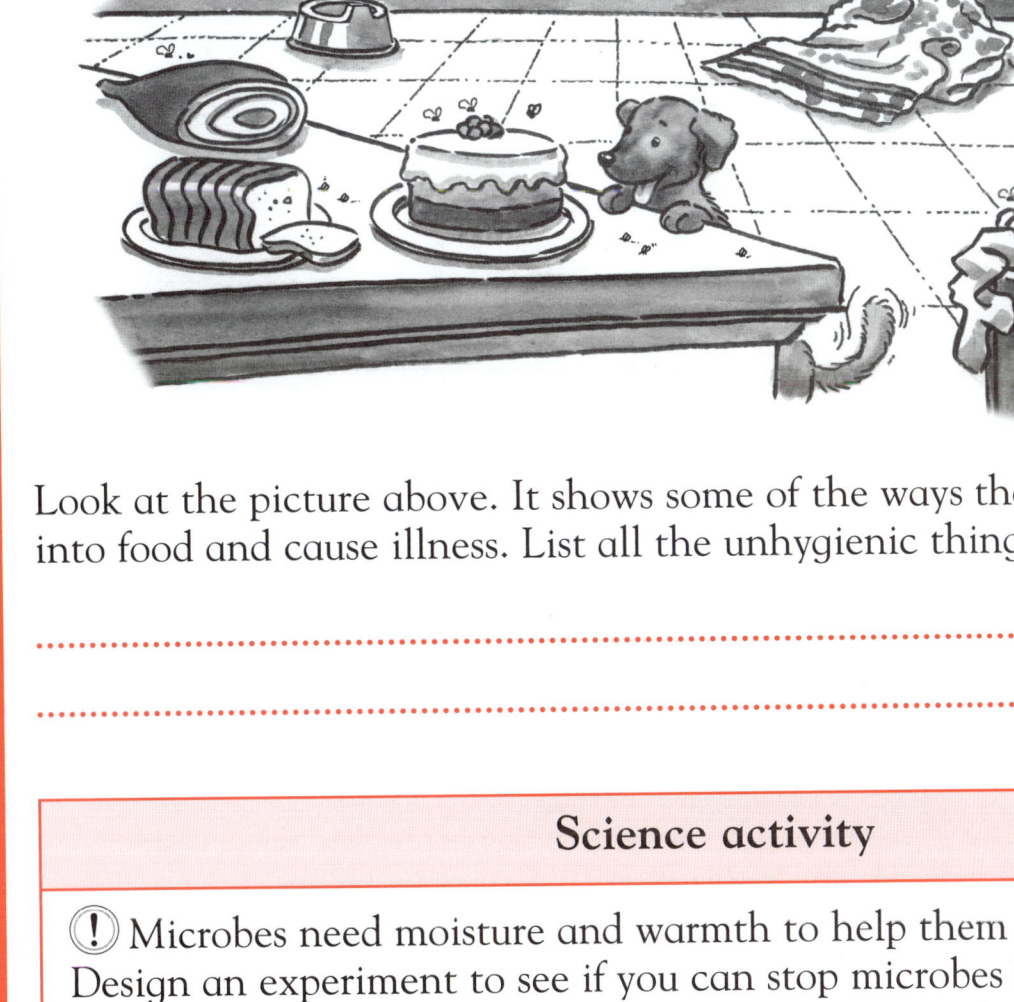

Look at the picture above. It shows some of the ways that germs can get into food and cause illness. List all the unhygienic things you can see.

....

....

Science activity

(!) Microbes need moisture and warmth to help them grow. Design an experiment to see if you can stop microbes from growing on bread. Remember to wash and dry your hands before and after this experiment.

How does the heart work?

Science facts

The heart is an organ located near the centre of the chest, within the protective ribcage. The heart pumps oxygen-carrying blood around the body. Its muscular walls contract and squeeze the blood out, forcing it into blood vessels that carry it to every part of the body. You can feel a throbbing sensation when you place your fingers on the side of your neck or on your wrist where the blood surges through blood vessels close to the surface of the skin. This throbbing is called your pulse.

Science quiz

This picture of the body has four heart shapes. Colour the heart shape that represents the position of the heart.

Science activity

You can feel your pulse by pressing your first two fingers against the top of your neck (underneath your jaw). Count how many times it beats in a minute. This is your pulse rate. Measure the pulse rate of other people. Is everyone's pulse rate the same? What could be the cause of any differences you observe?

What carries the blood?

Science facts

The heart pumps blood to all parts of the body. The blood pumped out of the heart is rich in oxygen. After supplying oxygen to the cells in the body, the blood returns to the heart. This continuous movement of blood is called circulation. Vessels carrying blood away from the heart are called arteries. Those carrying blood back to the heart are called veins. An artery has thicker walls than a vein because it has to withstand more pressure.

Science quiz

Fill in the missing letters in the labels for this diagram.

Blood going from heart to l _ _ _ _

B _ _ _ _ going from l _ _ _ _ to h _ _ _ _

Heart

Lung

Main v _ _ _

Main a _ _ _ _ _ _

Blood going from body to h _ _ _ _

B _ _ _ _ going from h _ _ _ _ to b _ _ _

Blood vessels in the body

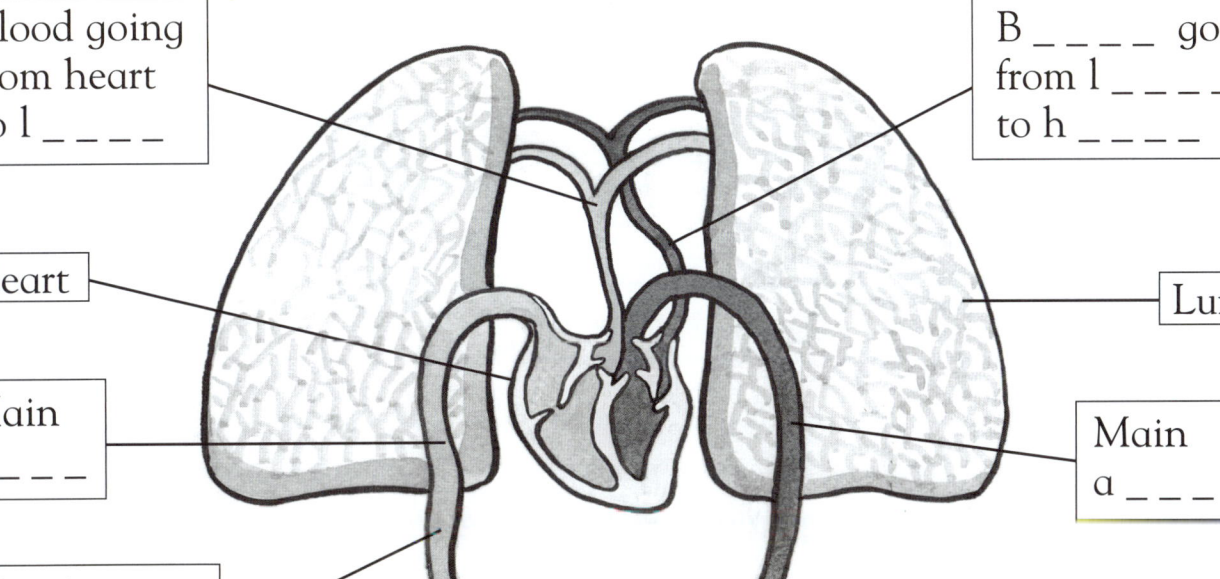

Science activity

Look at the veins in your lower arm and wrist. They look like thin blue lines under your skin. Can you see where the veins branch? Look at other people's arms. Is the pattern the same? Is there a difference between the veins of older people and those of children?

 # What happens when you exercise?

Science facts

Your heart contracts to push blood around your body. These contractions are called heartbeats. You can feel your heartbeat, or pulse, by placing a finger across blood vessels close to the surface of your skin. Your pulse rate is a measure of how many times your heart beats in one minute. When you exercise, your muscles work harder and need more oxygen-carrying blood. Exercise makes the pulse rate go up to increase the flow of blood to the muscles.

Science quiz

Angela measured her pulse rate after one minute, two minutes, three minutes and four minutes of exercise. She plotted her results on this graph.

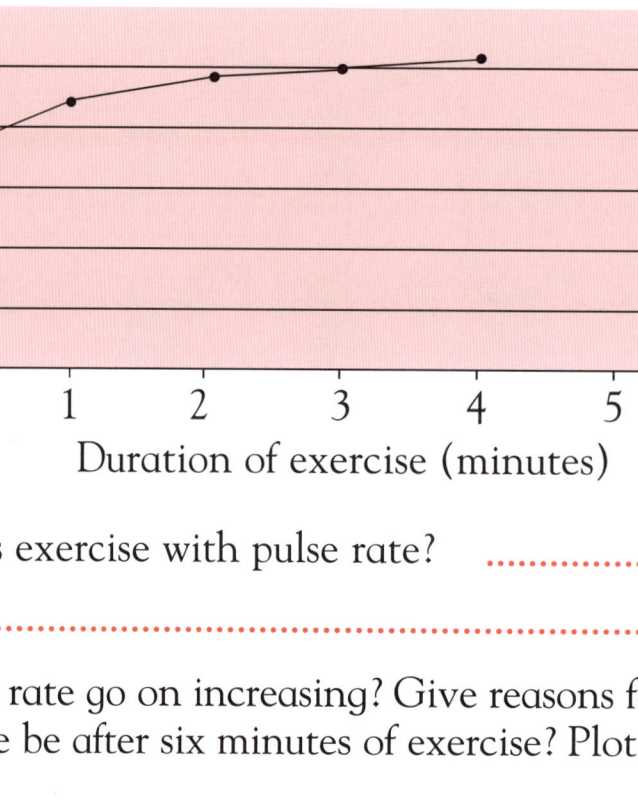

What pattern links exercise with pulse rate? ....

....

Can Angela's pulse rate go on increasing? Give reasons for your answer. What would her pulse rate be after six minutes of exercise? Plot this on the graph.

....

Science activity

⚠ Check your pulse rate and note it down. Now do an exercise, such as skipping, for one minute. Check your pulse rate again. How long does it take for your pulse to go back to normal? Repeat the experiment, first exercising for two minutes and then for three minutes. Plot a graph of your results.

What is in our food?

Science facts

Food is needed for growth, energy and health. You get energy by eating foods containing carbohydrates (sugars and starches) or fats. These foods include cakes, puddings, sweets, breads, potatoes and rice. Foods that provide you with the raw materials for growth and repair are rich in a substance called protein. These foods include meat, fish, eggs and beans. Some foods, such as fruits and vegetables, contain vitamins and minerals that keep you healthy by helping your body make full use of other foods.

Science quiz

Write the name of each food under the correct heading in the table below.

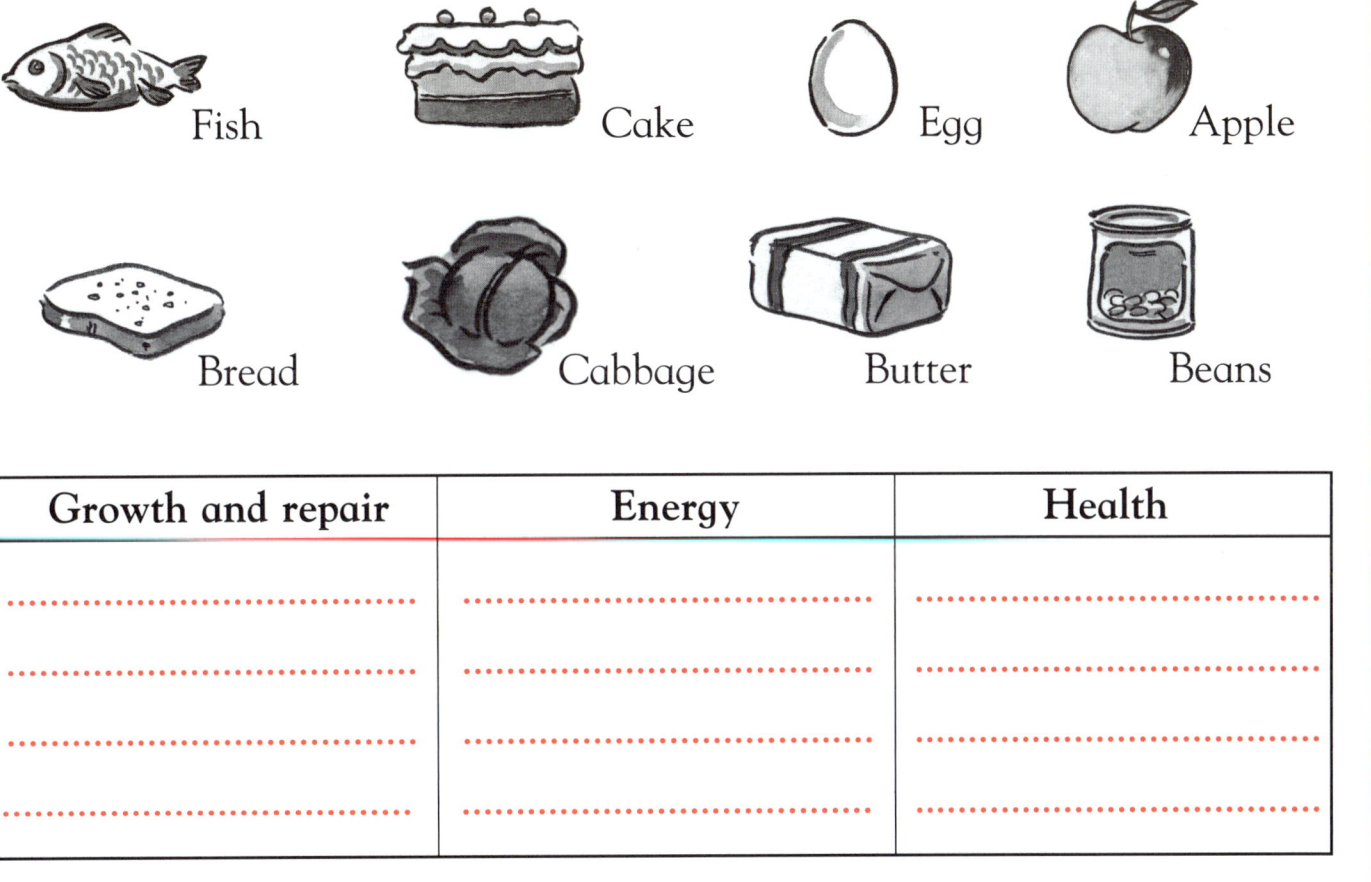

Fish   Cake   Egg   Apple

Bread   Cabbage   Butter   Beans

Growth and repair	Energy	Health
....	....	....
....	....	....
....	....	....
....	....	....

Science activity

Keep a record of what you eat over two days. Make a table like the one above and put the name of each food into the right group. Remember some foods can go under more than one heading. For example, the pastry in a meat pie gives you energy, while the meat helps growth.

Is your diet balanced?

Science facts

A healthy diet is a balanced combination of food for growth and repair, energy-giving food and some vitamins and minerals, which help the body work properly. You also need foods that contain fibre, which is found in green vegetables and whole grains. The amount of energy-giving food you need depends on how active you are and how much you are growing. Eating too much can make you overweight. Eating too little can cause tiredness and, in extreme cases, can lead to starvation.

Science quiz

Here are some meals with an item missing from each one. Decide what food item you would add to make each meal part of a balanced diet. Write the name of the item and which food group it is from.

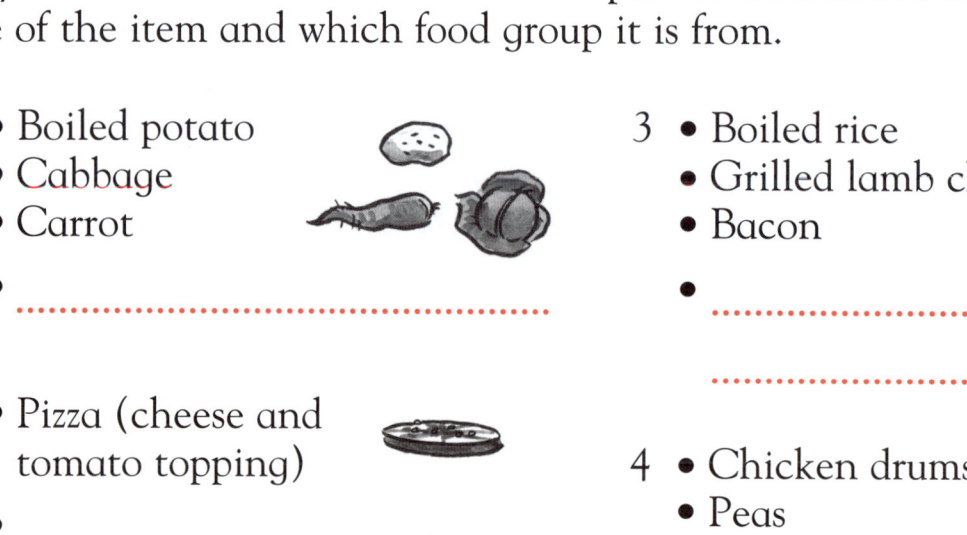

1 • Boiled potato
  • Cabbage
  • Carrot

  • ....

2 • Pizza (cheese and tomato topping)

  • ....
    ....

3 • Boiled rice
  • Grilled lamb chop
  • Bacon

  • ....
    ....

4 • Chicken drumsticks
  • Peas

  • ....

5 • Lettuce
  • Spring onions
  • Grated carrots
  • Bread

  • ....

6 • Fried egg
  • Bacon
  • Toast
  • Pudding

  • ....
    ....

Science activity

Collect some pictures of food from magazines and put them together to make a collage of a healthy dinner. Stick the pictures on some paper plates. Make a label for each food group. Stick the labels above the right pictures.

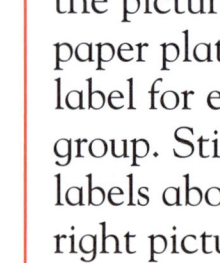

What are drugs?

Science facts

Medicines help you feel better when you are ill. A doctor or pharmacist tells you how much medicine you should take. Medicines contain drugs, which have an effect on the body. Alcohol and the nicotine in cigarettes are also drugs, but they are not medicines. In fact, they can harm or even kill you. Some drugs, such as heroin, cannabis and cocaine, are considered so harmful that it is against the law to own or sell them.

Science quiz

Which of these drugs would you normally get from a chemist's shop or a pharmacy? Put a tick (✔) by each one.

Wine

Cough medicine

Indigestion medicine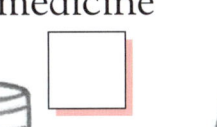

Beer

Headache pills

Eye drops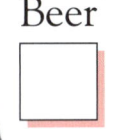

Antiseptic cream

Cigarettes

Science activity

(!) Ask an adult to show you the health warning on a packet of cigarettes. What are the dangers of smoking? Is the warning always the same on every brand of cigarette?

Are all drugs harmful?

Science facts

A drug is a chemical that affects the working of the body. Medicines are drugs that can be helpful when taken in controlled quantities (doses) following a doctor or pharmacist's instructions. Other drugs can be harmful. Nicotine is a drug that is found in tobacco. Smoking cigarettes can cause cancer and other serious diseases. Alcohol is also a drug that, in large quantities, can cause life-threatening diseases.

Science quiz

On the label of most medicines it says: "Keep out of reach of children". Explain why this instruction is important.

....

....

....

....

Science activity

Many pharmacists and doctors have leaflets about the dangers of smoking tobacco and drinking alcohol. Collect some of these and use the information on them to make your own poster listing the harmful effects of these drugs.

Are plants and animals similar?

Science facts

Like animals, plants need water, warmth, air and nutrients to live. They grow, reproduce, move and respond to things in the environment, such as sunlight and water. However, while animals need to find their food (plants or other animals), plants can make their own food using the green substance in their leaves. Plants stay rooted in the ground, but they can move their stems and leaves. Many plants reproduce by forming seeds, which grow into small plants. They do not lay eggs like fish, reptiles, birds and amphibians do or give birth to live young like mammals do.

Science quiz

These numbered words and phrases are features of plants and animals. Write the numbers under the correct heading in the chart below (some phrases are true for both animals and plants).

1 Move   2 Sensitive   3 Move over the ground
4 Grow   5 Make food   6 Form seeds
7 Reproduce   8 Need air   9 Eat
10 Need nutrients   11 Need sunlight   12 Lay eggs or have live young

Animals		Plants	
....	....	....	....
....	....	....	....
....	....	....	....
....	....	....	....
....	....	....	....

Science activity

(!) Plant a sunflower seed in a pot. Water it and keep it in a warm place. Watch it grow. At the beginning of summer, plant it in the garden or in a larger pot. How does it change during the day and from one day to the next? How is it different from a pet animal? Is it easier to look after? Why?

What are fossils?

Science facts

A fossil is the remains of a plant or animal that has been preserved in rock. There are different types of fossil: footprints and plants can make impressions, or indents, in rock. Shells, skeletons and teeth can be preserved in rock.

Science quiz

Read the list of different types of fossil given below. Draw a line between the name of each type of fossil and the correct picture.

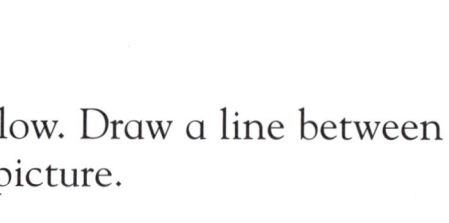

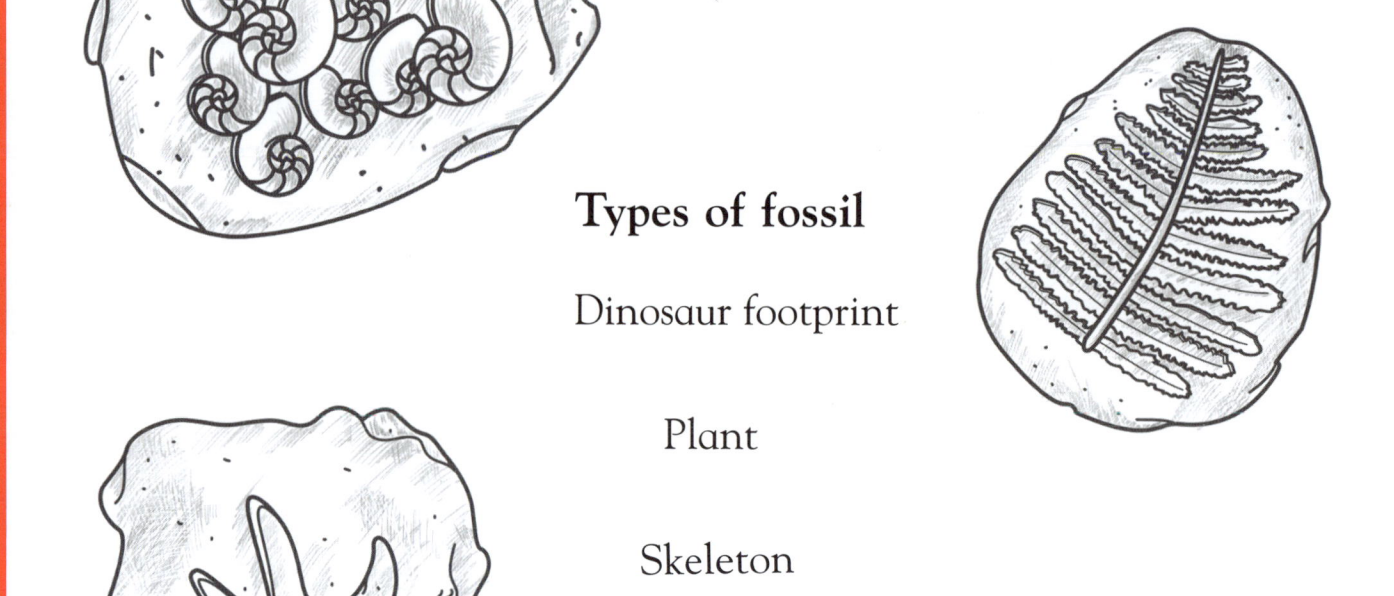

Types of fossil

Dinosaur footprint

Plant

Skeleton

Shells

Teeth

How have animals adapted?

Science facts

Animals come in many different shapes and sizes. Most animals live in one type of habitat because they are suited to it. We say they are adapted to the environment in which they live. For example, squirrels have sharp claws to grip and long tails to help them balance as they race up and down trees.

Science quiz

Look at these pictures. Explain how each animal has adapted to its habitat.

A mole burrows in dark underground tunnels.

A frog lives in ponds among the weeds.

A polar bear lives in the snowy Arctic.

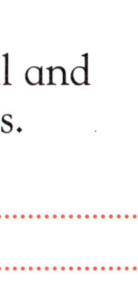

An owl is nocturnal and lives in the trees.

How do adaptations help?

Science facts

An adaptation is a feature that helps living things survive in the habitat they live in.

Science quiz

Read the sentences and match them to the correct animal by putting the number in the box. We have done the first one for you.

1 This animal's keen sense of hearing helps it detect prey at night.

2 This strong animal catches its prey with its sharp claws and strong jaws.

3 This animal uses its long tail to help it climb trees and cling to branches.

4 This animal has teeth strong enough to cut down trees to build dams.

5 This animal has a beak with a pouch so it can scoop up fish from the water.

6 This animal has a long neck so it can eat leaves high up in the trees.

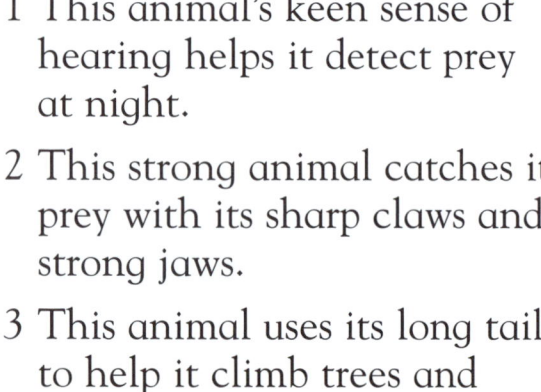

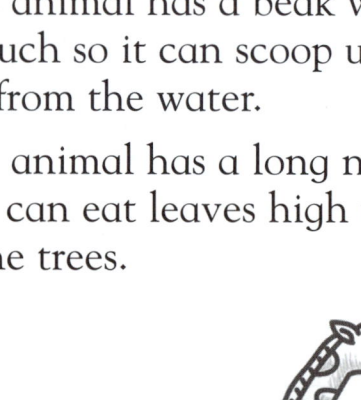

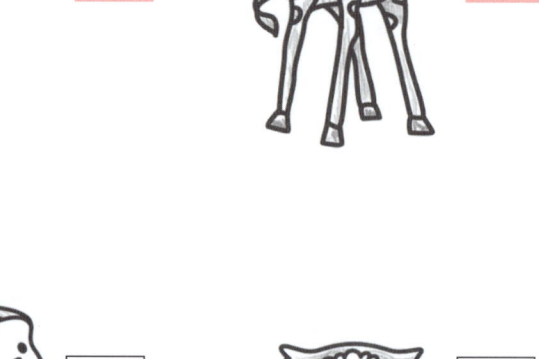

Who do you look like?

Science facts

A trait is a distinguishing characteristic – the way something looks or behaves. Scientists study traits to understand how living things are related.

Science quiz

Write your name at the top of the second column and the names of two members of your family at the top of the other columns. Record the age, height and other traits about you and your family members.

Traits	Relative	Your name	Relative
Age			
Male or female			
Height			
Eye colour			
Hair colour			
Shoe size			

Compare the information.

What traits do you share with your relatives?

....

....

....

What traits are different?

....

....

....

How does light travel?

Science facts

Light sources, such as the Sun, light bulbs and candles, give off light. Light travels in straight lines at a very fast speed. It travels much faster than sound. This is why we see the lightning in a storm before we hear the thunder.

Science quiz

A lit candle was placed behind a wall.

Why could it not be seen on this side of the wall?

....

....

At the end of a long field, a man was hammering a stake into the ground. From the other end of the field, people could see him hit the stake before they heard the sound of the hammer. Explain why this happened.

....

....

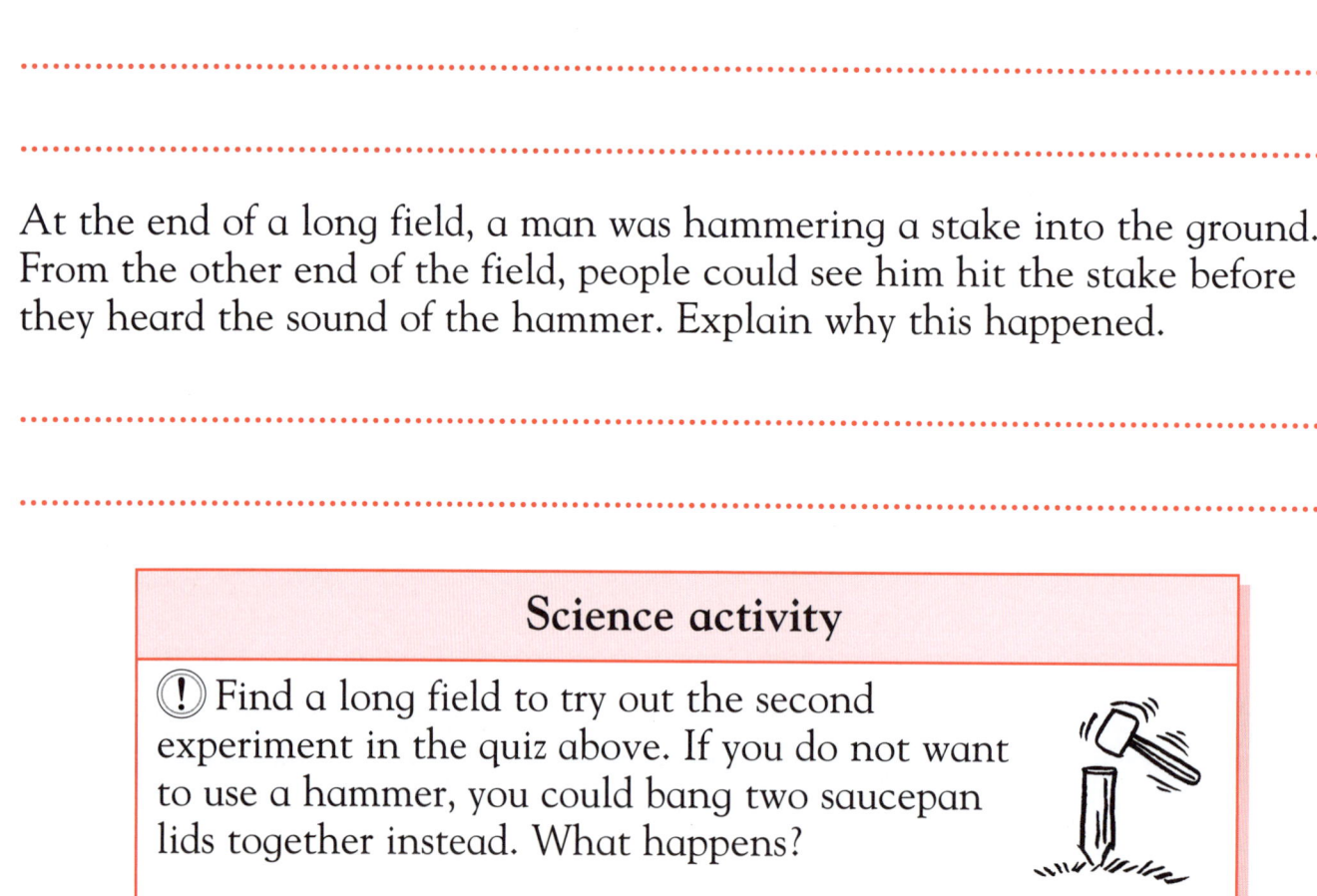

Science activity

(!) Find a long field to try out the second experiment in the quiz above. If you do not want to use a hammer, you could bang two saucepan lids together instead. What happens?

How can we see around corners?

Science facts

When light bounces off a surface, we say it is reflected. Shiny surfaces reflect light well. Light always travels in straight lines and is reflected in straight lines. When a ray of light hits a mirror at an angle, it is reflected at the same angle. If a light ray hits a mirror at 45°, it is reflected at 45°. If an object is placed in the path of the light ray, its image could be seen by someone who may not see the actual object (see diagram below).

Object   Wall   Person

Light ray   Light ray

45°   45°

Mirror

Science quiz

A class made some periscopes to see over a hedge. A diagram of a periscope is shown below. One light ray has been drawn for you. Complete the diagram by drawing two more light rays to show how the light is reflected from the mirrors into the eye.

Light ray →

Mirror

Mirror

Science activity

Have a look at the back of your head.
You will need two mirrors to do this.
At what angle do you need to hold the mirrors to see the side of your head?

How do we see things?

Science facts

A lighted candle, a torch and the Sun are all sources of light. We see them because light travels from them and enters our eyes.

We see other things around us, such as a book, a table or a wall, because light from a light source reflects off their surfaces and enters our eyes.

Science quiz

Sam can see both the light bulb and the chair. Draw arrows to show how the light from the bulb travels so that he can see both.

Science activity

(!) In a darkened room, place a candle on one side of a large book and a small object, such as a toy, on the other side. Does the candle light up the object? Now remove the book and look again. How does this prove that light does not come from your eyes but bounces off the object and enters your eyes?

What are the sources of light?

Science facts

Light enables us to see a bright and colourful world. Light travels in straight lines called rays. Light bulbs and the Sun are sources of light. They make light. Mirrors and many other objects reflect light. They do not make light.

Science quiz

Look at the pictures and put a tick (✔) in the correct box to indicate if it is a source of light or if it reflects light.

	Source of light	Reflects light
Safety strips	☐	☐
Firefly	☐	☐
Moon	☐	☐
Candle	☐	☐
Television	☐	☐

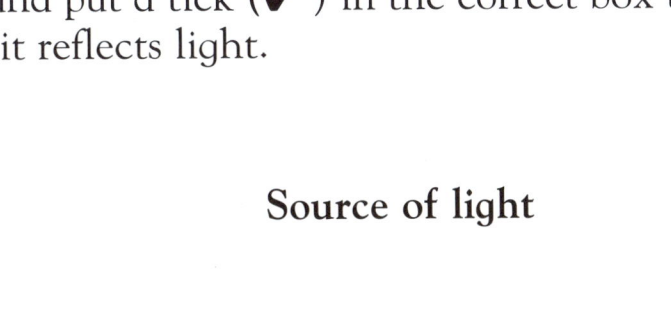

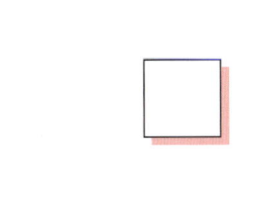

What reflects light?

Science facts

When rays of light hit a smooth, shiny surface, they are reflected back. The flat surface of a mirror, for example, gives a perfect, clear image. Light also reflects off the surface of water.

Science quiz

(!) Using the objects pictured below, carry out the six instructions and record your results.

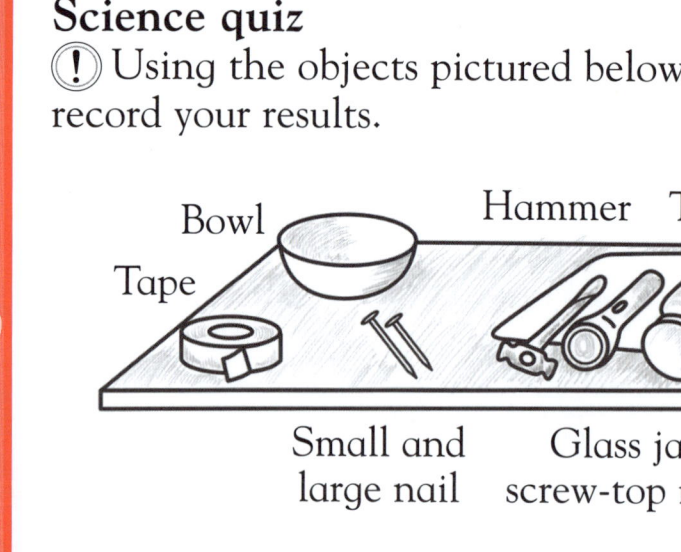

Tape Bowl Hammer Torch Newspaper

Small and large nail Glass jar with screw-top metal lid

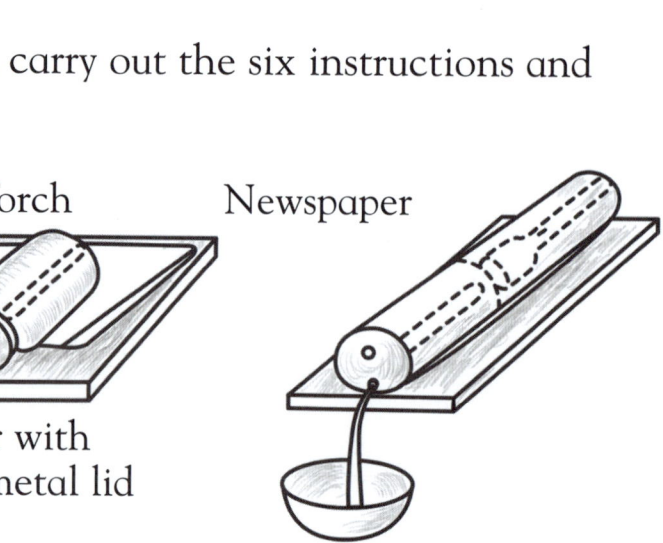

1 Use the hammer and the nail to make a small hole in the lid of the jar near one edge and a larger hole near the opposite edge. Ask an adult to help you.

2 Fill the jar with water and then screw the top back on tightly. Cover the holes with tape.

3 Lay the jar lengthwise at one end of the newspaper.

4 Turn on the torch. Position it at the bottom end of the glass jar so that its light shines through the jar.

5 Roll up the jar and the torch (turned on) in the newspaper so that the newspaper forms a tube around them.

6 Turn off the room light so that it is dark. Remove the tape from the holes in the lid and watch the water pouring out of the jar into the bowl.

What do you notice about the streams of water?

....

....

What do you think is happening?

....

....

What are the parts of the eye?

Science facts

The human eye has many parts. Light enters the eye through an opening called the pupil. The coloured part around the pupil is called the iris. The cornea and lens work together to focus light onto the retina – a layer of light-sensitive cells at the back of the eye. The cells pick up the pattern of light and send signals to the brain along the optic nerve to form the image that we see.

Science quiz

Look at the picture and use the words in the box to complete the sentences.

Cornea	Iris	Lens	Optic nerve	Pupil	Retina

Lens

Iris

Pupil

Cornea

Retina

Optic nerve

Cross-section of the eye

1 The .... is a clear layer at the front of the eyeball.

2 The .... is a ring of coloured tissue around the pupil.

3 The .... is a hole that lets light into the eye.

4 The .... is a curved structure that bends light rays entering the eye.

5 The .... is a layer of cells at the back of the eye that detects light.

6 The .... sends messages from the eye to the brain.

Will it form a shadow?

Science facts

You can see clearly through some materials because light travels straight through them; they are called transparent materials. Other materials allow only some light to go through them; they are called translucent materials. Materials that allow no light to pass through them are called opaque materials. A shadow is formed when an opaque or translucent object blocks the light.

Science quiz

Use a black pencil or pen to draw in the shadows in this picture.

Science activity

Collect a few objects made from different materials, such as a glass beaker, a china plate and a plastic jug. Predict which objects will allow the most light through and which will allow the least.
To check your predictions, shine a torch on each object in a darkened room. Check how much light shines through the object onto a white paper screen placed on the other side.

What affects the size of a shadow?

Science facts

Light travels in straight lines. It radiates out in all directions from a light source. When an object blocks the light, a shadow is formed. The shadow will get bigger if the light source is moved closer to the object. Moving the object farther away from its shadow will also make the shadow bigger.

Science quiz

John was making a shadow-puppet theatre. He used a sheet stretched between two table legs as his screen and a bright lamp as his light source. He made the shape of a person from cardboard and stuck it on a stick, but the shadow of the shape was too big for the screen.

How could he make the shadow smaller? List two ways.

....

....

Science activity

Find out how you can make a shadow bigger. Use a bottle or a book as your object, a torch as your light source and a wall as your screen. You will need a tape measure or a ruler to measure the size of the shadow. How big can you make the shadow? How small can you make it? How did you change the size of the shadow?

What do batteries do?

Science facts

Batteries are a source of electricity. They are made up of one or more 1.5-V units, called cells. (V stands for volt, which is a measure of how much energy a battery has.) A 3-V battery is made of two 1.5-V cells linked together. A battery has two ends called the positive (+) and negative (−) poles. Wires must be connected to these poles for electric current to flow in a circuit. Adding more batteries to a circuit increases the flow of electricity, making the current greater. The brightness of a bulb is a measure of the amount of electric current in the circuit. A brighter bulb indicates greater electric current.

Science quiz

The drawings below show two electric circuits.

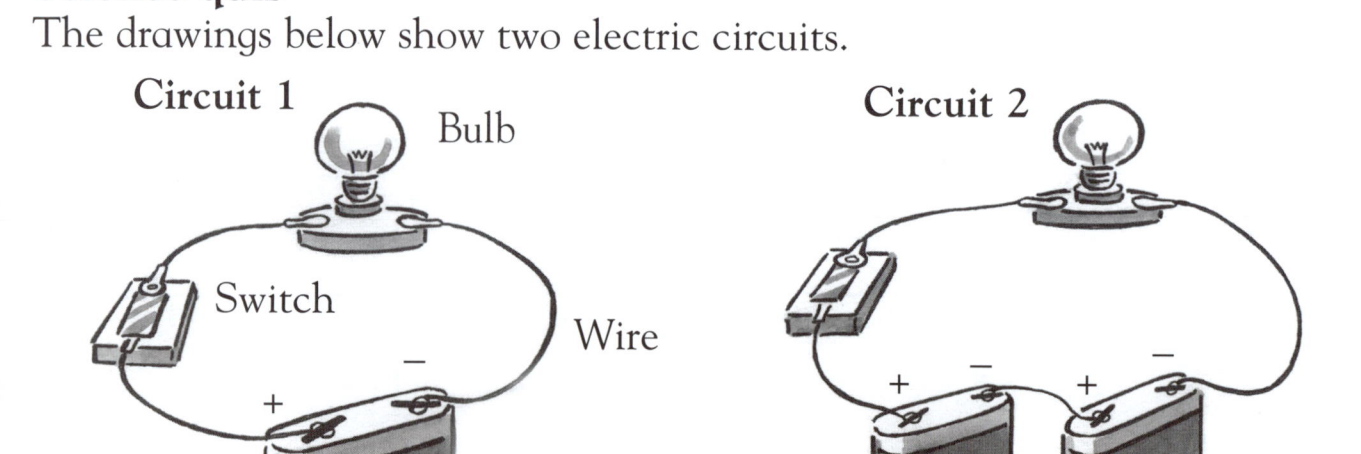

What is the difference between these two circuits?

....

In which circuit is the bulb brighter when the switch is closed? Why?

....

....

Science activity

Make a torch using a cardboard tube, a battery, some wires, a bulb and a switch. Add another battery, making sure that you connect one battery's positive pole to the other's negative pole. Add a third battery. When is the bulb the brightest?

Do more bulbs mean more light?

Science facts

Inside a light bulb, there is a thin wire called a filament. When electricity flows through this filament, some of the electrical energy is changed into light energy. The flow of electricity, or the electric current, is slower when there is a bulb in a circuit. If another bulb is added, the current slows down even more and the filaments in each bulb do not glow as brightly.

Science quiz

Dipak made the circuit shown below. He was surprised that the bulbs were so dim that they were hardly glowing. He did not have another battery, so how do you think he could have changed the circuit to make the light brighter?

....

....

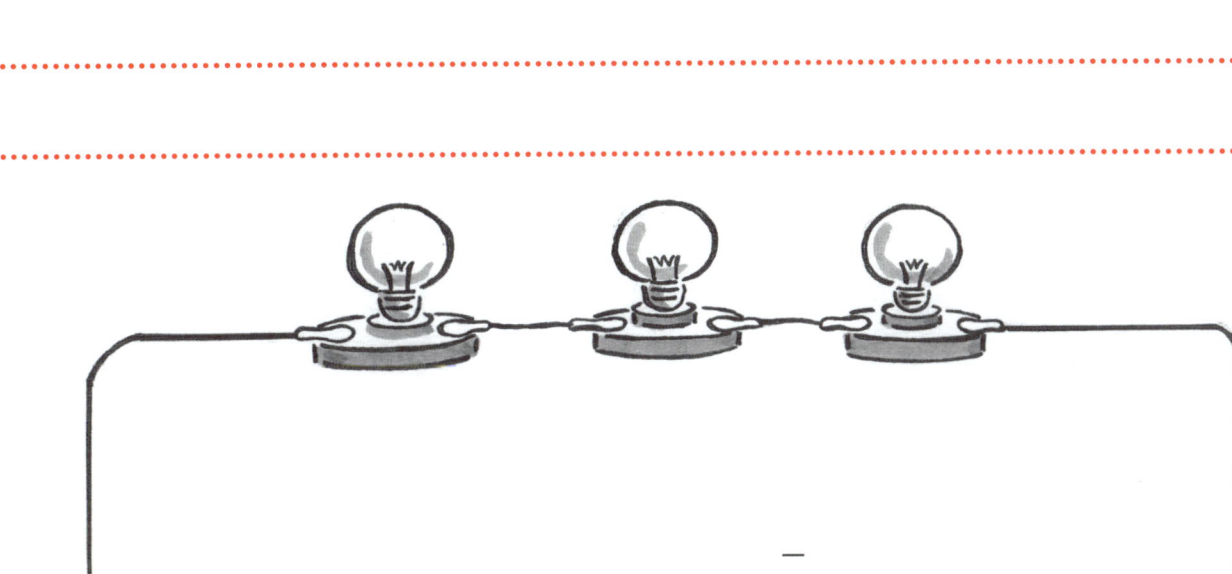

Science activity

Make a circuit with two bulbs a battery, a switch and four strips of wire. How can you change the circuit to increase the brightness of one bulb?

What does a circuit diagram show?

Science facts

Electricity always flows around a circuit in one direction – from the negative (–) pole of a battery to the positive (+) pole. This flow of electricity is called the electric current. Electrical circuits can be represented by special diagrams. There is a symbol for each electrical component in a circuit.

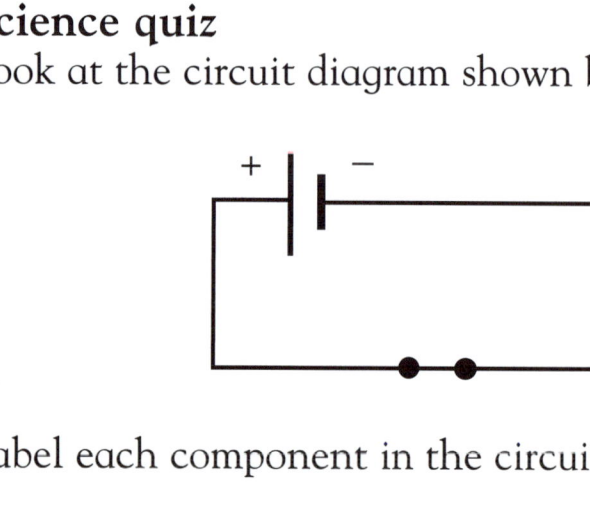

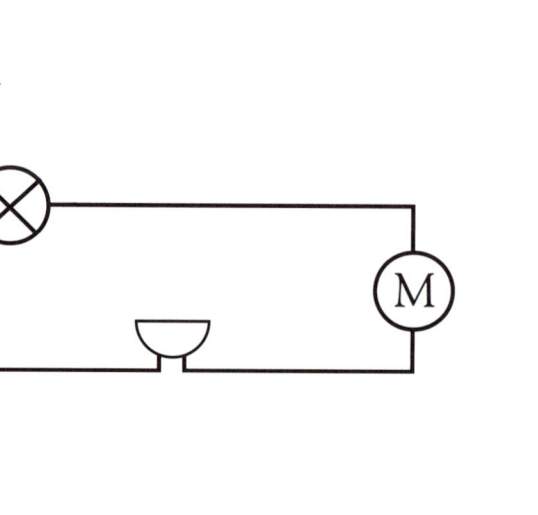

Science quiz

Look at the circuit diagram shown below.

Label each component in the circuit.

Complete the missing words in the following sentence about the circuit above.

The electric current leaves the battery and first passes through the .... ,

next it travels through the .... , then through the ....

and finally through the .... , before returning to the battery.

Science activity

Draw some symbols of electrical components on different cards. Using lines to represent wires, arrange the cards to make a circuit. With your finger, trace the path of electricity around the circuit from one end of the battery to the other.

Can you draw a circuit diagram?

Science facts

A simple circuit diagram is usually set out as a rectangle. It shows how the components, such as bulbs, switches, batteries and wires are linked in a circuit.

Science quiz

Look at these two pictures of circuits.

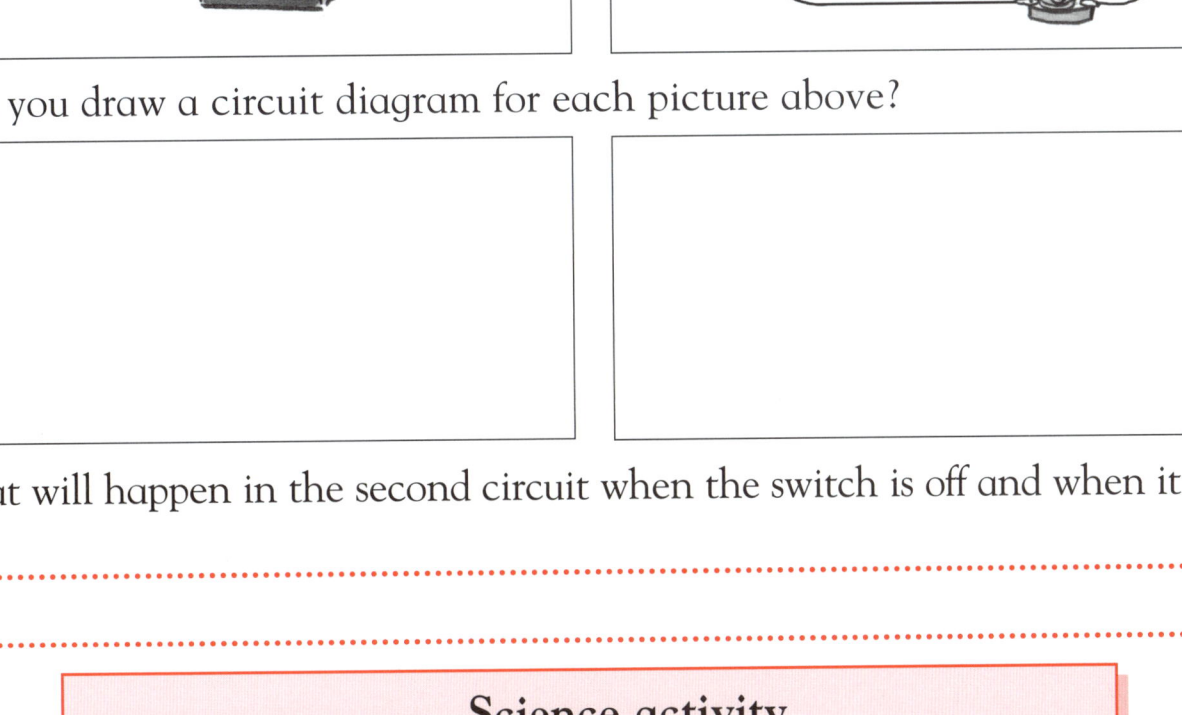

Can you draw a circuit diagram for each picture above?

What will happen in the second circuit when the switch is off and when it is on?

....

....

Science activity

(!) This is the circuit diagram for a game. The aim is to pass the wire loop along the curved wire without touching it. Touching it will sound the buzzer. Make the curved shape from coat-hanger wire. Strip the plastic off some insulated wire to make the loop, but do not strip the loop handle.

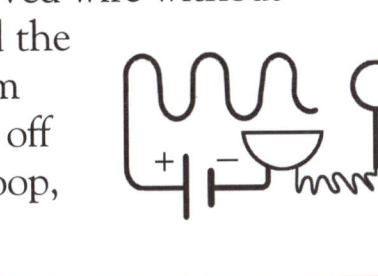

Will it switch on or off?

Science facts

Electricity will flow in a circuit only if there are no breaks in it. A switch is a useful device because you can use it to make a break in a circuit and stop the electricity flowing whenever you want. You use switches to turn electric lights and other household appliances on and off.

This is the symbol for an open switch. —•⁄•— This switch is off.
This is the symbol for a closed switch. —•—•— This switch is on.

This switch is closed by
pressing down the metal bar.

This switch is closed by turning
the lever and slotting it into the clip.

Science quiz

Look at this circuit diagram.

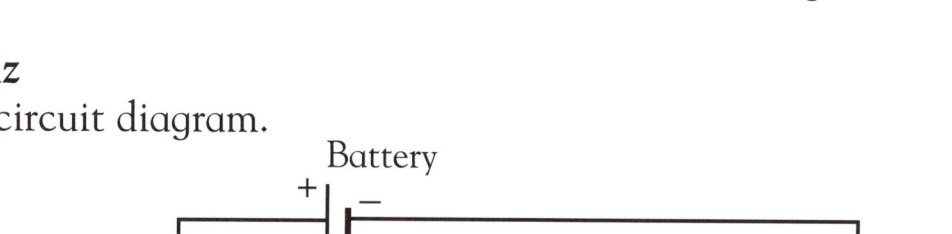

What is the least number of switches you
need to close to make the bulb light up? ....

Which switches are they? ....

Science activity

Make a pressure switch using two sheets of aluminium foil slightly separated by a few balls of cotton wool. Use this in a circuit with a battery and a buzzer to make a burglar alarm. When the two sheets touch each other, the switch closes and the circuit is completed. What happens when you step on your pressure switch? _____

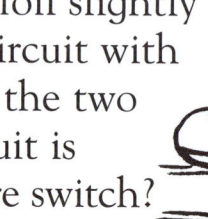

Answer Section with Parents' Notes
Key Stage 2
Ages 10–11

This section provides answers and explanatory notes to the quizzes and activities in the book. Work through each page together and ensure that your child understands each task. Point out any mistakes in your child's work and correct any errors, but also remember to praise your child's efforts and achievements. Where appropriate, ask your child to predict the outcome of the *Science activity* experiments. After each experiment, challenge your child to explain the results.

(!) If a *Science activity* box includes this caution symbol, extra care is necessary. In such cases, experiments may involve heavy weights, sharp objects, hot water, ice or soil. Always wear gloves when handling soil and ensure hands are washed afterwards. Gloves are also advisable for activities in which hot or very cold objects are used.

 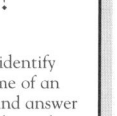 ## What kind of animal is this?

Science facts
There are many different species of animal. Scientists use keys to identify them. Being able to use keys is an important skill. To find the name of an animal, you can use a branching key. Start at the top of the key and answer **Yes** or **No** to each question. Follow the branches until you reach the end.

Science quiz
Arthropods are small animals with jointed legs. The word **arthropod** means "jointed legs".

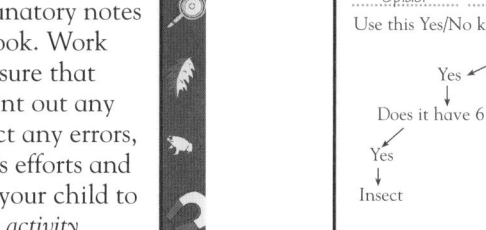

Spider   Millipede   Insect   Centipede   Crustacean

Use this Yes/No key to identify each type of arthropod shown above.

Does it have 8 legs or less?
- Yes → Does it have 6 legs?
  - Yes → Insect
  - No → Spider
- No → Does it have two pairs of antennae?
  - Yes → Crustacean
  - No → Does it have one pair of legs per segment?
    - Yes → Centipede
    - No → Millipede

> **Science activity**
>
> You will need some gloves and tweezers for this activity. In autumn, collect some leaf litter (damp, dead leaves) and spread it out on some newspaper. Carefully examine it using the tweezers. Can you find any arthropods? Use the key above to identify them.

Your child will learn how to use a branching key to identify different arthropods. When collecting leaf litter, ensure your child wears gloves to avoid infection. He or she should study any creatures on a saucer before returning them safely to the wild.

What sort of plant is this?

Science facts
Trees are plants. There are many different types, or species, of tree. Based on observable characteristics, branching keys can be used to identify different species.

Science quiz
Look at the pictures of the four twigs below. Use the key to identify each one. Write your answers on the dotted lines.

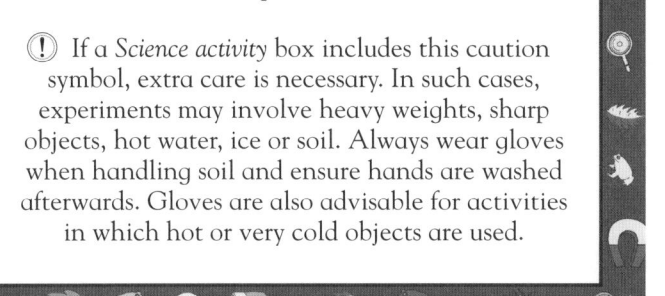

.... Ash .... Horse chestnut ....

.... Beech .... Oak ....

Do the buds grow in opposite pairs?
- Yes → Are the buds black, small and pointed?
  - Yes → Ash
  - No → Horse chestnut
- No → Are the buds long and thin?
  - Yes → Beech
  - No → Oak

> **Science activity**
>
> In spring, collect different types of twig. Examine the buds carefully. Can you make a key to help identify different species?

Encourage your child to collect twigs from familiar trees. Look carefully at the differences in bud shape, length and texture (for example, horse chestnut buds are sticky). Help your child compile a key to identify the twigs.

Can you make a bird key?

Science facts
Branching keys work best when things are divided into groups and then further divided into smaller groups. When putting birds into groups, you could first divide them into wading birds (those with webbed feet) and non-wading birds and then think of some subsets, such as size, shape or colour of beak.

Science quiz

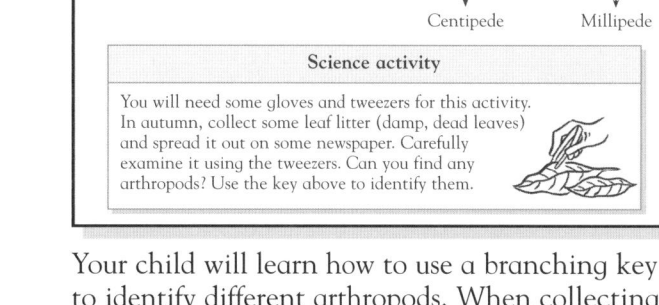

Swan   Blackbird   Duck   Moorhen   Magpie

Make a branching key for the birds above using their different characteristics.

Answers may vary

> **Science activity**
>
> Birds that often visit gardens and parks include the thrush, starling, sparrow, blue tit, robin, wren, crow and rook. Leave some scraps of bread or nuts on the ground in your garden or local park. Which birds come to eat them? Make a key for these birds.

Your child will learn how to construct a branching key to distinguish between different birds. Make sure the questions are suitable and based on clear differences (e.g., "Does the bird have a yellow beak?" is better than "Does it have a yellow beak?").

Can you make a plant key?

Science facts
Yes/No keys can also be written as numbered questions. Answer the questions below to identify the three plants in the pictures.

1 Is the plant over 2 metres tall?
   If yes, go to 2; if no, go to 3.
2 It is an oak tree.
3 Does the plant have a flower?
   If yes, go to 4; if no, go to 5.
4 It is a daffodil.
5 It is moss.

Science quiz
Make a Yes/No key to distinguish between the different flowers shown below.

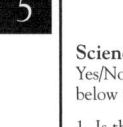

Iris

....
....
....
....
....

Rose

....
....
....

Daffodil

Science activity
Look at some plants in your garden or local park. Can you make a Yes/No key to identify them? Ask some friends to try your key. Does it work?

Here, your child will learn how to make a Yes/No key to identify plants. The secret is to pinpoint clear differences. Good keys will identify a plant in one step. Test your child's key and discuss any improvements that could be made.

How do microbes help?

Science facts
Microbes, or micro-organisms, are living things that are often too small to be seen. Three common types of microbes are bacteria, viruses and some fungi. These organisms need food, warmth and moisture to grow and reproduce. Some microbes feed on things that were once living, such as fallen leaves and dead animals, causing them to break down, or decay. The decayed materials mix with the soil, providing essential nutrients for plants to use. Without this process, the nutrients in the soil would run out. Microbes also help us make some of our foods, such as bread, cheese, yogurt, beer and wine. They feed on the sugar in grain, fruit or milk, giving these foods a special texture and taste.

Science quiz
Zarine put the following items into a large polythene bag. She took them out again after two weeks. In the boxes below, write **D** for the items that would have decayed and **U** for those that would be unchanged.

D Grass	D Tangerine
U Plastic spoon	U Bread
D Apple peel	D Leaves
U Cola can	U Nylon tights

Why have some of the items not decayed?

Microbes can only feed on things that were once living. They cannot eat metal or plastic.

Science activity
To grow microbes, mix one teaspoon of dried yeast and half a teaspoon of sugar in half a cup of slightly warm water. Add enough of this mixture to 125 grams of flour to make the grains stick together. Make a ball from the dough and place it on a plate in a warm place. What happens?

Your child will learn that some microbes provide nutrients for plants and are important in making some foods. Yeast is a microbe: it eats sugar and produces a gas. In bread-making, the gas forms bubbles in the dough, causing it to rise.

How are microbes harmful?

Science facts
Some microbes, often called germs, can cause illness or disease. Chickenpox, mumps and measles are caused by microbes. They are infectious diseases. Some microbes can cause food to decay. Mouldy bread or fruit, rotten meat and sour milk are examples of decayed food. If eaten, this rotten food and drink can cause stomach upsets. Other microbes cause tooth decay. You can protect yourself from harmful microbes by storing and preparing food properly, cleaning your teeth, washing your hands and by not coming in close contact with ill people.

Science quiz

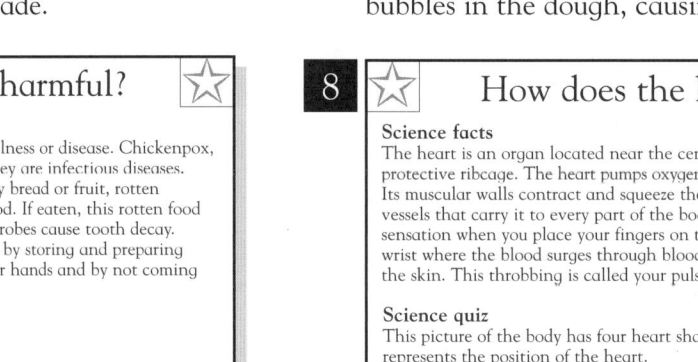

Look at the picture above. It shows some of the ways that germs can get into food and cause illness. List all the unhygienic things you can see.

Uncovered rubbish attracts flies, which spread germs to uncovered food.

The dog, dirty laundry and potty could all carry germs.

Science activity
⚠ Microbes need moisture and warmth to help them grow. Design an experiment to see if you can stop microbes from growing on bread. Remember to wash and dry your hands before and after this experiment.

Your child will learn that microbes, or "germs", can also make people ill. Discuss basic rules of hygiene with your child. To stop microbes growing on bread, your child could try drying it, keeping it cool, freezing it or putting it in an airtight bag.

How does the heart work?

Science facts
The heart is an organ located near the centre of the chest, within the protective ribcage. The heart pumps oxygen-carrying blood around the body. Its muscular walls contract and squeeze the blood out, forcing it into blood vessels that carry it to every part of the body. You can feel a throbbing sensation when you place your fingers on the side of your neck or on your wrist where the blood surges through blood vessels close to the surface of the skin. This throbbing is called your pulse.

Science quiz
This picture of the body has four heart shapes. Colour the heart shape that represents the position of the heart.

Science activity
You can feel your pulse by pressing your first two fingers against the top of your neck (underneath your jaw). Count how many times it beats in a minute. This is your pulse rate. Measure the pulse rate of other people. Is everyone's pulse rate the same? What could be the cause of any differences you observe?

The heart pumps blood around the body through arteries and veins. If your child can't feel the pulse in the wrist, try the one in the neck. Count for 30 seconds and multiply by 2 to find the pulse rate. Pulse rate is affected by age, health and exercise.

What carries the blood?

Science facts

The heart pumps blood to all parts of the body. The blood pumped out of the heart is rich in oxygen. After supplying oxygen to the cells in the body, the blood returns to the heart. This continuous movement of blood is called circulation. Vessels carrying blood away from the heart are called arteries. Those carrying blood back to the heart are called veins. An artery has thicker walls than a vein because it has to withstand more pressure.

Science quiz

Fill in the missing letters in the labels for this diagram.

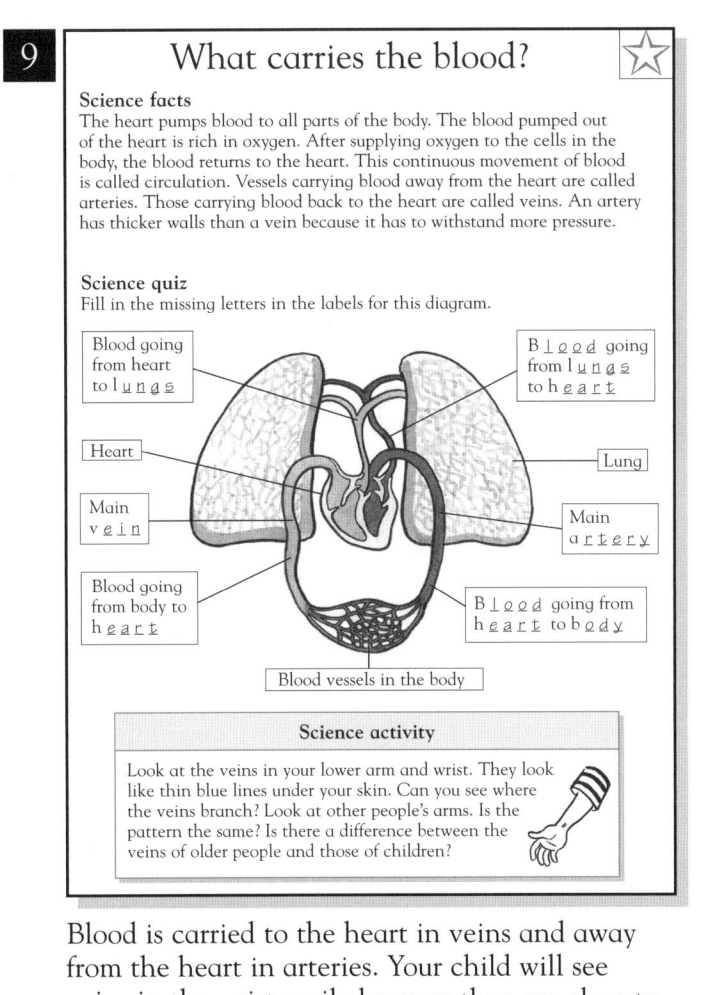

Blood going from heart to l u n g s

B l o o d going from l u n g s to h e a r t

Heart

Lung

Main v e i n

Main a r t e r y

Blood going from body to h e a r t

B l o o d going from h e a r t to b o d y

Blood vessels in the body

Science activity

Look at the veins in your lower arm and wrist. They look like thin blue lines under your skin. Can you see where the veins branch? Look at other people's arms. Is the pattern the same? Is there a difference between the veins of older people and those of children?

Blood is carried to the heart in veins and away from the heart in arteries. Your child will see veins in the wrist easily because they are close to the surface. Ensure your child notices how veins branch to collect blood from all over the body.

What happens when you exercise?

Science facts

Your heart contracts to push blood around your body. These contractions are called heartbeats. You can feel your heartbeat, or pulse, by placing a finger across blood vessels close to the surface of your skin. Your pulse rate is a measure of how many times your heart beats in one minute. When you exercise, your muscles work harder and need more oxygen-carrying blood. Exercise makes the pulse rate go up to increase the flow of blood to the muscles.

Science quiz

Angela measured her pulse rate after one minute, two minutes, three minutes and four minutes of exercise. She plotted her results on this graph.

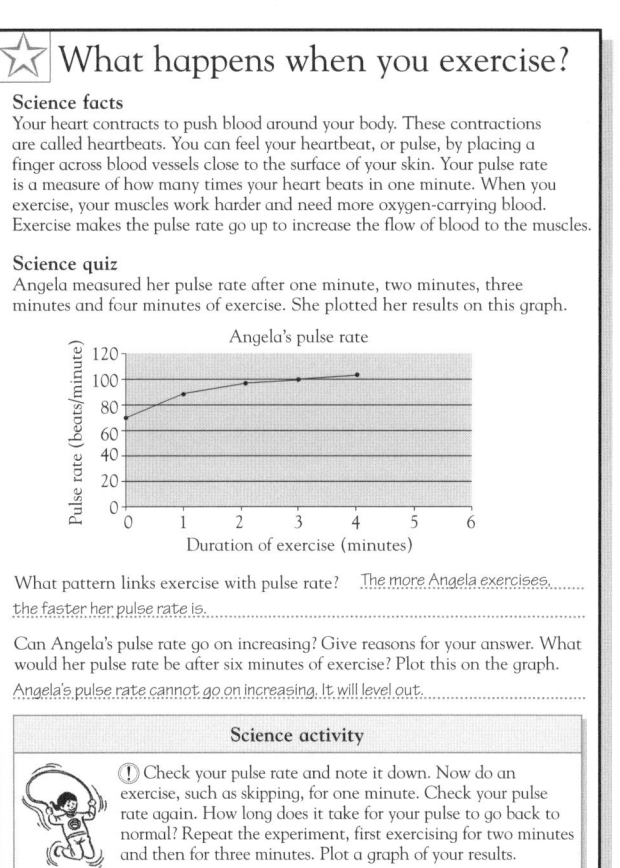

Angela's pulse rate

Pulse rate (beats/minute) / Duration of exercise (minutes)

What pattern links exercise with pulse rate? The more Angela exercises, the faster her pulse rate is.

Can Angela's pulse rate go on increasing? Give reasons for your answer. What would her pulse rate be after six minutes of exercise? Plot this on the graph.

Angela's pulse rate cannot go on increasing. It will level out.

Science activity

⚠ Check your pulse rate and note it down. Now do an exercise, such as skipping, for one minute. Check your pulse rate again. How long does it take for your pulse to go back to normal? Repeat the experiment, first exercising for two minutes and then for three minutes. Plot a graph of your results.

Children with breathing or other medical problems should avoid the skipping activity. If your child asks about the increase in breathing rate with exercise, explain that this happens to raise oxygen levels as blood is pumped faster to the muscles.

What is in our food?

Science facts

Food is needed for growth, energy and health. You get energy by eating foods containing carbohydrates (sugars and starches) or fats. These foods include cakes, puddings, sweets, breads, potatoes and rice. Foods that provide you with the raw materials for growth and repair are rich in a substance called protein. These foods include meat, fish, eggs and beans. Some foods, such as fruits and vegetables, contain vitamins and minerals that keep you healthy by helping your body make full use of other foods.

Science quiz

Write the name of each food under the correct heading in the table below.

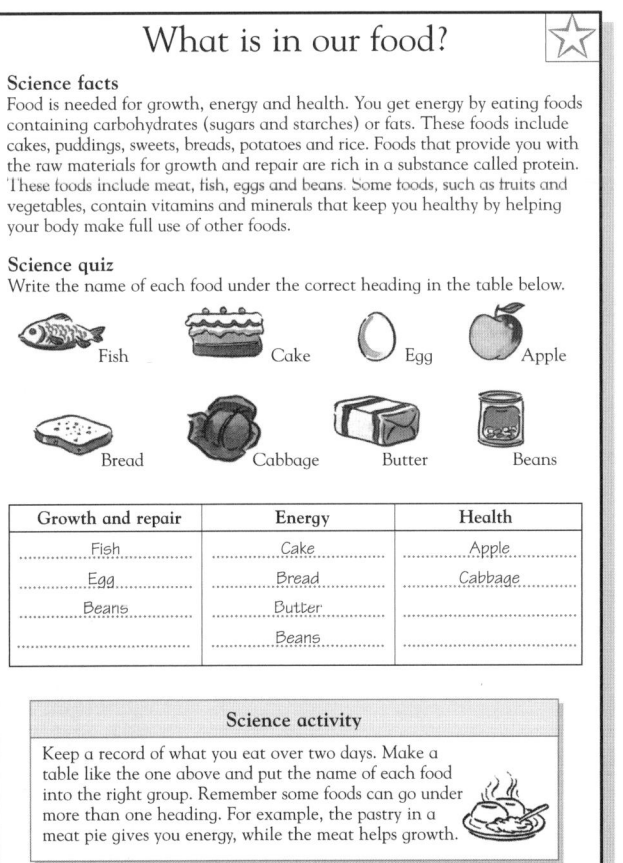

Fish   Cake   Egg   Apple

Bread   Cabbage   Butter   Beans

Growth and repair	Energy	Health
Fish	Cake	Apple
Egg	Bread	Cabbage
Beans	Butter	
	Beans	

Science activity

Keep a record of what you eat over two days. Make a table like the one above and put the name of each food into the right group. Remember some foods can go under more than one heading. For example, the pastry in a meat pie gives you energy, while the meat helps growth.

Meat, fish, etc. (proteins) help growth and repair; potatoes, sweets, etc. (fats and carbohydrates) provide energy; and fruits and vegetables containing vitamins and minerals aid health. Some foods, such as beans, contain both protein and carbohydrate.

Is your diet balanced?

Science facts

A healthy diet is a balanced combination of food for growth and repair, energy-giving food and some vitamins and minerals, which help the body work properly. You also need foods that contain fibre, which is found in green vegetables and whole grains. The amount of energy-giving food you need depends on how active you are and how much you are growing. Eating too much can make you overweight. Eating too little can cause tiredness and, in extreme cases, can lead to starvation.

Science quiz Answers may vary

Here are some meals with an item missing from each one. Decide what food item you would add to make each meal part of a balanced diet. Write the name of the item and which food group it is from.

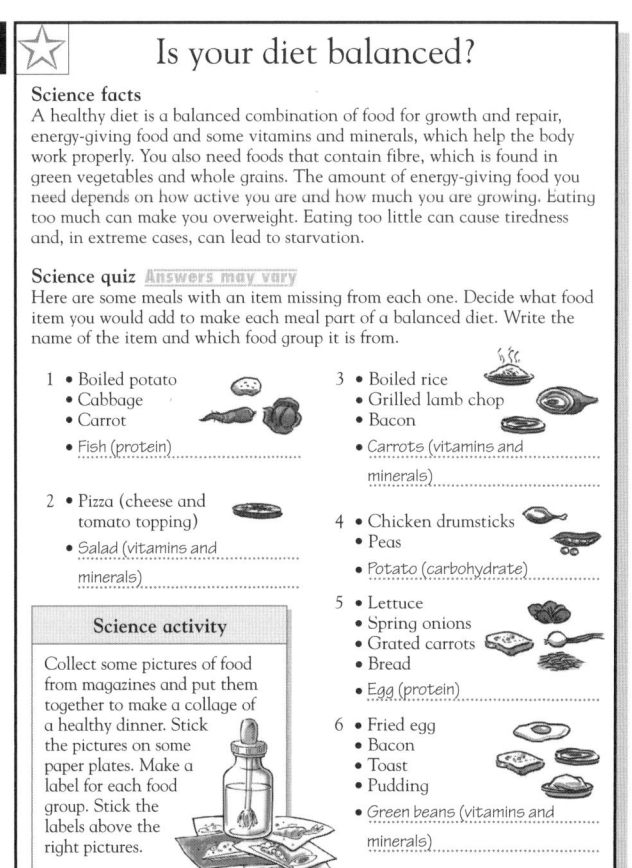

1 • Boiled potato
  • Cabbage
  • Carrot
  • Fish (protein)

2 • Pizza (cheese and tomato topping)
  • Salad (vitamins and minerals)

3 • Boiled rice
  • Grilled lamb chop
  • Bacon
  • Carrots (vitamins and minerals)

4 • Chicken drumsticks
  • Peas
  • Potato (carbohydrate)

5 • Lettuce
  • Spring onions
  • Grated carrots
  • Bread
  • Egg (protein)

6 • Fried egg
  • Bacon
  • Toast
  • Pudding
  • Green beans (vitamins and minerals)

Science activity

Collect some pictures of food from magazines and put them together to make a collage of a healthy dinner. Stick the pictures on some paper plates. Make a label for each food group. Stick the labels above the right pictures.

A healthy diet means eating the right types of food in the right amounts. Help your child ensure that there is one growth food (meat, fish, eggs, beans, cheese), one energy food (potato, rice, pastry) and one health food (vegetables, fruit) in each meal.

What are drugs?

Science facts
Medicines help you feel better when you are ill. A doctor or pharmacist tells you how much medicine you should take. Medicines contain drugs, which have an effect on the body. Alcohol and the nicotine in cigarettes are also drugs, but they are not medicines. In fact, they can harm or even kill you. Some drugs, such as heroin, cannabis and cocaine, are considered so harmful that it is against the law to own or sell them.

Science quiz
Which of these drugs would you normally get from a chemist's shop or a pharmacy? Put a tick (✔) by each one.

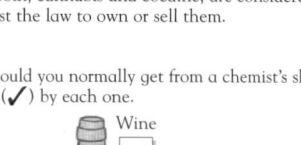
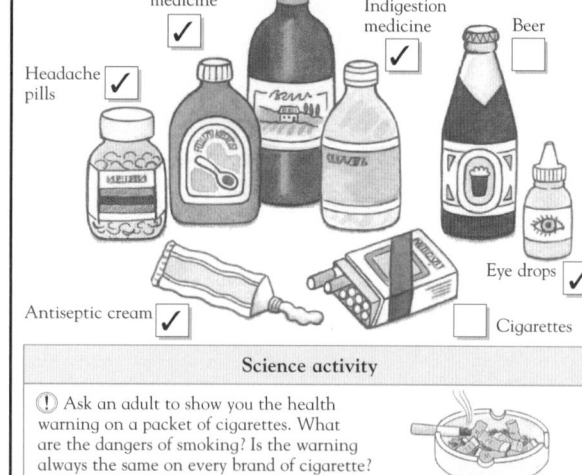

Wine ☐

Cough medicine ✔

Indigestion medicine ✔

Beer ☐

Headache pills ✔

Eye drops ✔

Antiseptic cream ✔

Cigarettes ☐

Science activity
⚠ Ask an adult to show you the health warning on a packet of cigarettes. What are the dangers of smoking? Is the warning always the same on every brand of cigarette?

The idea that all medicines are drugs but not all drugs are medicines is an important one. Encourage your child to collect information on drugs from a doctor's surgery or health centre. Discuss the effects of drugs and their use and abuse with your child.

Are all drugs harmful?

Science facts
A drug is a chemical that affects the working of the body. Medicines are drugs that can be helpful when taken in controlled quantities (doses) following a doctor or pharmacist's instructions. Other drugs can be harmful. Nicotine is a drug that is found in tobacco. Smoking cigarettes can cause cancer and other serious diseases. Alcohol is also a drug that, in large quantities, can cause life-threatening diseases.

Science quiz
On the label of most medicines it says: "Keep out of reach of children". Explain why this instruction is important.

This instruction is important because children may think that these pills are sweets and eat them. Too much asprin or paracetamol can be harmful. It is important for adults to administer medicines to children in the correct dosage.

Science activity
Many pharmacists and doctors have leaflets about the dangers of smoking tobacco and drinking alcohol. Collect some of these and use the information on them to make your own poster listing the harmful effects of these drugs.

Your child will learn about the role of drugs and their effects on the body. Remind your child to ask before taking medication. Discuss the problems associated with drinking and smoking, and talk about the dangers of taking narcotic drugs.

Are plants and animals similar?

Science facts
Like animals, plants need water, warmth, air and nutrients to live. They grow, reproduce, move and respond to things in the environment, such as sunlight and water. However, while animals need to find their food (plants or other animals), plants can make their own food using the green substance in their leaves. Plants stay rooted in the ground, but they can move their stems and leaves. Many plants reproduce by forming seeds, which grow into small plants. They do not lay eggs like fish, reptiles, birds and amphibians do or give birth to live young like mammals do.

Science quiz
These numbered words and phrases are features of plants and animals. Write the numbers under the correct heading in the chart below (some phrases are true for both animals and plants).

1 Move	2 Sensitive	3 Move over the ground
4 Grow	5 Make food	6 Form seeds
7 Reproduce	8 Need air	9 Eat
10 Need nutrients	11 Need sunlight	12 Lay eggs or have live young

Animals		Plants	
1	8	1	7
2	9	2	8
3	10	4	10
4	12	5	11
7		6	

Science activity
⚠ Plant a sunflower seed in a pot. Water it and keep it in a warm place. Watch it grow. At the beginning of summer, plant it in the garden or in a larger pot. How does it change during the day and from one day to the next? How is it different from a pet animal? Is it easier to look after? Why?

Sunflowers are sensitive to the Sun and turn to face it. They are easy to plant and grow quickly. Observing them will reinforce for your child that like animals, plants also grow, reproduce, move and are sensitive to their environment.

What are fossils?

Science facts
A fossil is the remains of a plant or animal that has been preserved in rock. There are different types of fossil: footprints and plants can make impressions, or indents, in rock. Shells, skeletons and teeth can be preserved in rock.

Science quiz
Read the list of different types of fossil given below. Draw a line between the name of each type of fossil and the correct picture.

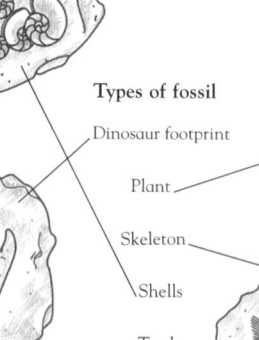

Types of fossil

Dinosaur footprint

Plant

Skeleton

Shells

Teeth

Discuss with your child what can be learned from a fossil of a footprint. We can guess how big or small the animal was or how old or young it was. We can guess by the shape of the footprint if the animal was a fast runner, a slow walker or a swimmer.

17 How have animals adapted? ⭐

Science facts
Animals come in many different shapes and sizes. Most animals live in one type of habitat because they are suited to it. We say they are adapted to the environment in which they live. For example, squirrels have sharp claws to grip and long tails to help them balance as they race up and down trees.

Science quiz
Look at these pictures. Explain how each animal has adapted to its habitat.

A mole burrows in dark underground tunnels.

Long claws help it dig. It only needs tiny eyes because it lives in the dark.

A frog lives in ponds among the weeds.

Webbed toes help it swim and its green colouring helps it hide from predators among the weeds.

A polar bear lives in the snowy Arctic.

Long, thick, white fur keeps it warm and hides it in the snow so it can creep up on prey.

An owl is nocturnal and lives in the trees.

Large eyes and good hearing help it hunt at night.

Ask your child how he or she thinks a shark and a chameleon are adapted to their environments. Ask him or her to think about body shape, colouring or camouflage and which senses or body parts they use to find food.

18 ⭐ How do adaptations help?

Science facts
An adaptation is a feature that helps living things survive in the habitat they live in.

Science quiz
Read the sentences and match them to the correct animal by putting the number in the box. We have done the first one for you.

1 This animal's keen sense of hearing helps it detect prey at night.

2 This strong animal catches its prey with its sharp claws and strong jaws.

3 This animal uses its long tail to help it climb trees and cling to branches.

4 This animal has teeth strong enough to cut down trees to build dams.

5 This animal has a beak with a pouch so it can scoop up fish from the water.

6 This animal has a long neck so it can eat leaves high up in the trees.

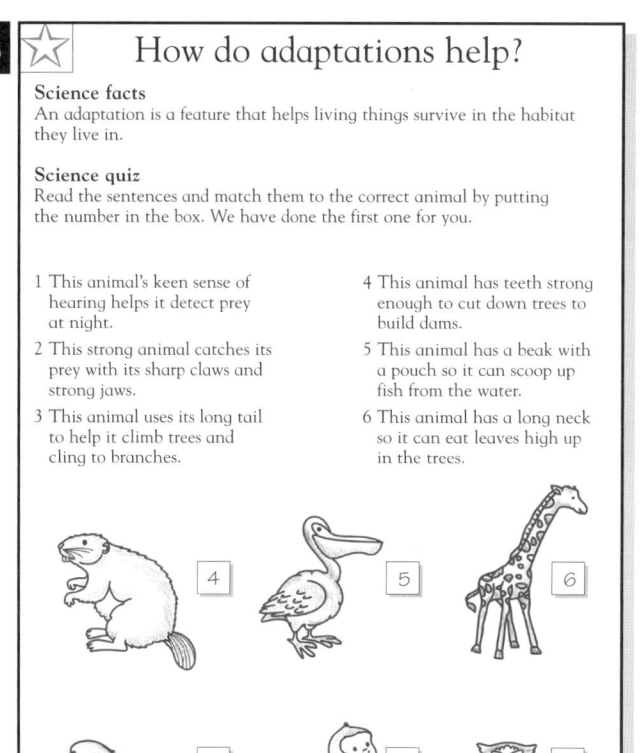

Behaviours are adaptations, too. For example, some animals are nocturnal. Why might they adapt to that kind of behaviour? (Possible answers: to hide from predators; to avoid the heat of the day and conserve water, especially in deserts.)

19 Who do you look like? ⭐

Science facts
A trait is a distinguishing characteristic – the way something looks or behaves. Scientists study traits to understand how living things are related.

Science quiz
Write your name at the top of the second column and the names of two members of your family at the top of the other columns. Record the age, height and other traits about you and your family members.

Traits	Relative	Your name	Relative
Age			
Male or female			
Height			
Eye colour			
Hair colour			
Shoe size			

Answers may vary

Compare the information. *Answers may vary*

What traits do you share with your relatives?

What traits are different?

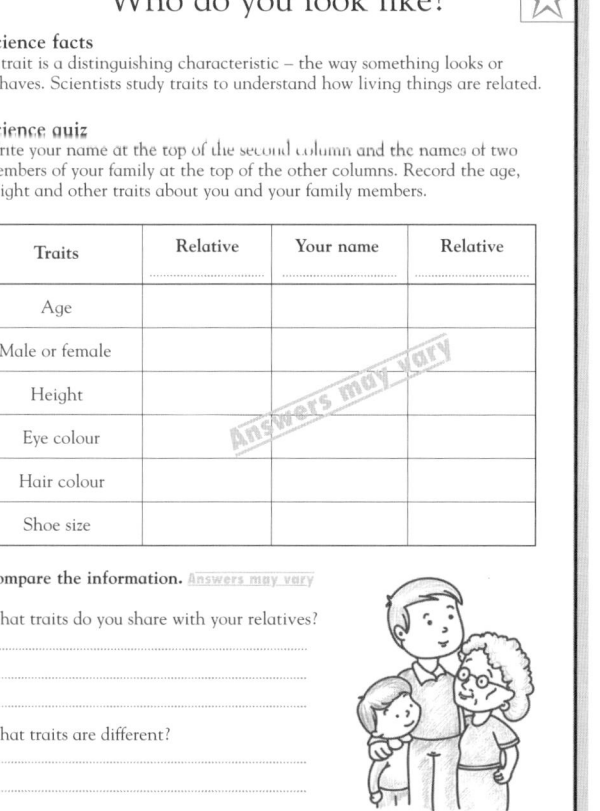

Have your child repeat this quiz with friends instead of relatives. Compare the results. Are friends more or less like your child than family members are?

20 ⭐ How does light travel?

Science facts
Light sources, such as the Sun, light bulbs and candles, give off light. Light travels in straight lines at a very fast speed. It travels much faster than sound. This is why we see the lightning in a storm before we hear the thunder.

Science quiz
A lit candle was placed behind a wall.

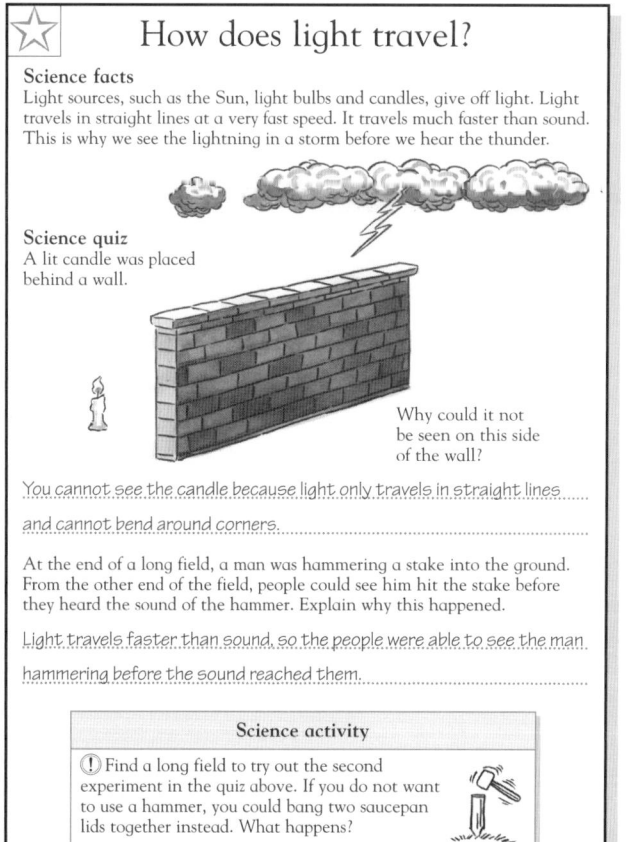

Why could it not be seen on this side of the wall?

You cannot see the candle because light only travels in straight lines and cannot bend around corners.

At the end of a long field, a man was hammering a stake into the ground. From the other end of the field, people could see him hit the stake before they heard the sound of the hammer. Explain why this happened.

Light travels faster than sound, so the people were able to see the man hammering before the sound reached them.

Science activity

⚠ Find a long field to try out the second experiment in the quiz above. If you do not want to use a hammer, you could bang two saucepan lids together instead. What happens?

The *Science activity* works well on a still day in a field about the length of a football pitch. To verify that sound travels more slowly than light, ask your child to raise one hand on seeing the object being struck and the other hand on hearing the sound.

21 How can we see around corners? ⭐

Science facts
When light bounces off a surface, we say it is reflected. Shiny surfaces reflect light well. Light always travels in straight lines and is reflected in straight lines. When a ray of light hits a mirror at an angle, it is reflected at the same angle. If a light ray hits a mirror at 45°, it is reflected at 45°. If an object is placed in the path of the light ray, its image could be seen by someone who may not see the actual object (see diagram below).

Science quiz
A class made some periscopes to see over a hedge. A diagram of a periscope is shown below. One light ray has been drawn for you. Complete the diagram by drawing two more light rays to show how the light is reflected from the mirrors into the eye.

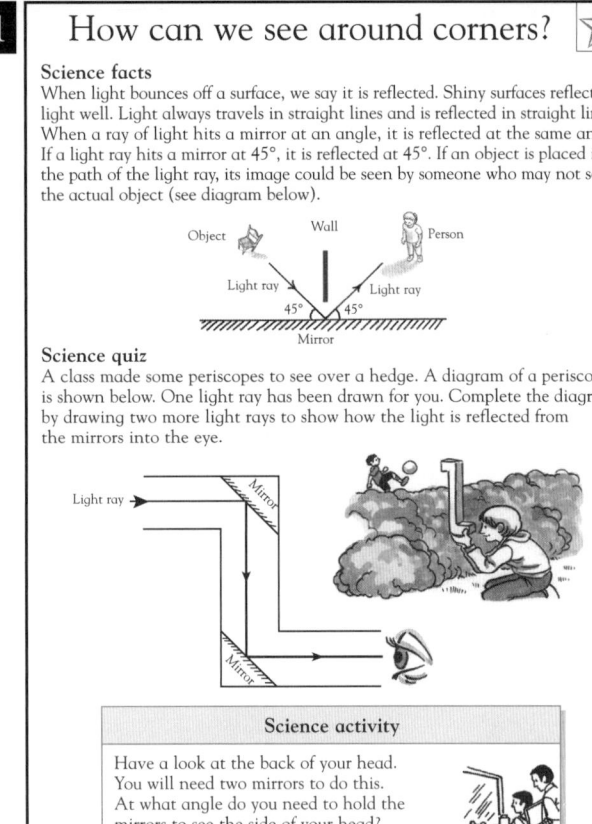

Science activity
Have a look at the back of your head. You will need two mirrors to do this. At what angle do you need to hold the mirrors to see the side of your head?

To prove that light can be reflected, help your child make a periscope using three cardboard tubes (from kitchen-towel rolls) and two small, plastic handbag mirrors. Cut slots in the cardboard and put the mirrors in at 45° angles.

22 ⭐ How do we see things?

Science facts
A lighted candle, a torch and the Sun are all sources of light. We see them because light travels from them and enters our eyes.

We see other things around us, such as a book, a table or a wall, because light from a light source reflects off their surfaces and enters our eyes.

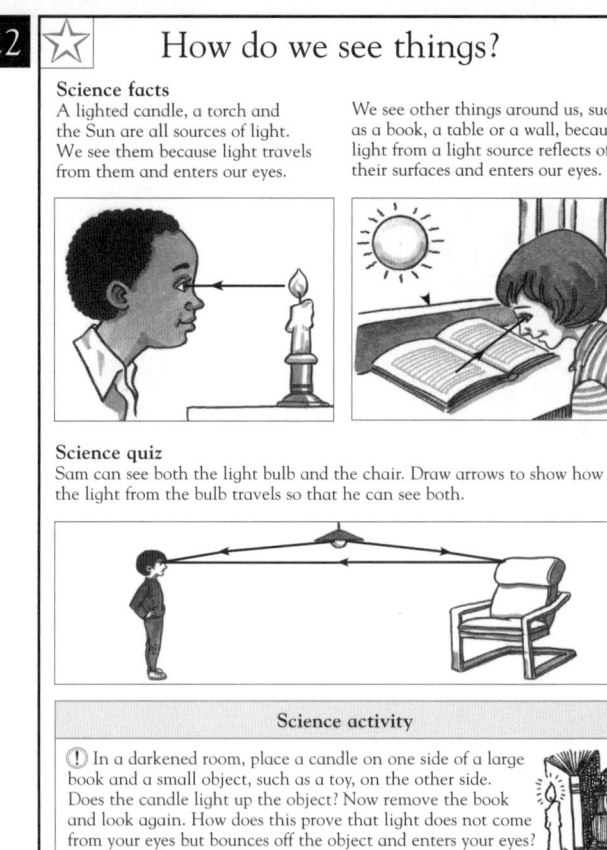

Science quiz
Sam can see both the light bulb and the chair. Draw arrows to show how the light from the bulb travels so that he can see both.

Science activity
⚠ In a darkened room, place a candle on one side of a large book and a small object, such as a toy, on the other side. Does the candle light up the object? Now remove the book and look again. How does this prove that light does not come from your eyes but bounces off the object and enters your eyes?

We see things because light is reflected off them. Children often think that only shiny objects reflect light. Another common misconception is that light comes from our eyes. Check that your child understands that this is not so.

23 What are the sources of light? ⭐

Science facts
Light enables us to see a bright and colourful world. Light travels in straight lines called rays. Light bulbs and the Sun are sources of light. They make light. Mirrors and many other objects reflect light. They do not make light.

Science quiz
Look at the pictures and put a tick (✔) in the correct box to indicate if it is a source of light or if it reflects light.

	Source of light	Reflects light
Safety strips		✔
Firefly	✔	
Moon		✔
Candle	✔	
Television	✔	

In bright light, we can see lots of detail and colour, while it is harder in dim light. Make your child read the same page in four different degrees of brightness, from almost dark to very bright. Let him or her record how easy or difficult it was each time.

24 ⭐ What reflects light?

Science facts
When rays of light hit a smooth, shiny surface, they are reflected back. The flat surface of a mirror, for example, gives a perfect, clear image. Light also reflects off the surface of water.

Science quiz
⚠ Using the objects pictured below, carry out the six instructions and record your results.

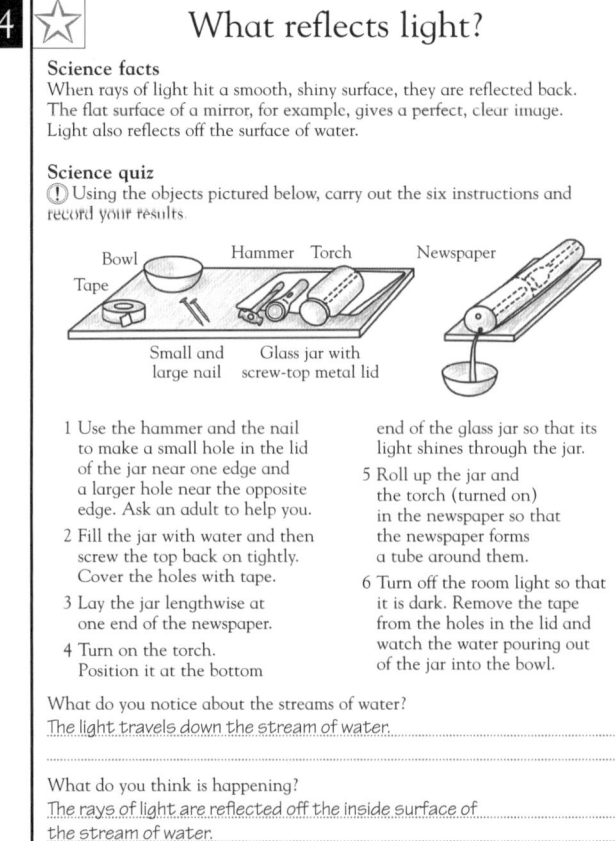

1 Use the hammer and the nail to make a small hole in the lid of the jar near one edge and a larger hole near the opposite edge. Ask an adult to help you.
2 Fill the jar with water and then screw the top back on tightly. Cover the holes with tape.
3 Lay the jar lengthwise at one end of the newspaper.
4 Turn on the torch. Position it at the bottom

end of the glass jar so that its light shines through the jar.
5 Roll up the jar and the torch (turned on) in the newspaper so that the newspaper forms a tube around them.
6 Turn off the room light so that it is dark. Remove the tape from the holes in the lid and watch the water pouring out of the jar into the bowl.

What do you notice about the streams of water?
The light travels down the stream of water.

What do you think is happening?
The rays of light are reflected off the inside surface of the stream of water.

Have your child set the torch (turned on) on the table in a darkened room. Let him or her pick an object in the room (a picture, chair, etc.) and try to aim the beam of light from the torch at that object using only a mirror. Can he or she do it?

What are the parts of the eye?

Science facts
The human eye has many parts. Light enters the eye through an opening called the pupil. The coloured part around the pupil is called the iris. The cornea and lens work together to focus light onto the retina – a layer of light-sensitive cells at the back of the eye. The cells pick up the pattern of light and send signals to the brain along the optic nerve to form the image that we see.

Science quiz
Look at the picture and use the words in the box to complete the sentences.

| Cornea | Iris | Lens | Optic nerve | Pupil | Retina |

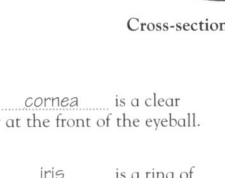
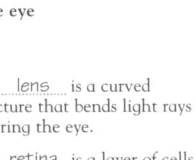

Retina
Lens
Iris
Pupil
Cornea
Optic nerve

Cross-section of the eye

1 The _cornea_ is a clear layer at the front of the eyeball.

2 The _iris_ is a ring of coloured tissue around the pupil.

3 The _pupil_ is a hole that lets light into the eye.

4 The _lens_ is a curved structure that bends light rays entering the eye.

5 The _retina_ is a layer of cells at the back of the eye that detects light.

6 The _optic nerve_ sends messages from the eye to the brain.

Explain to your child that the retina is home to two specialised types of cells: rods and cones. Rods are sensitive to light and allow us to see in dim light but not in colour. Cones allow us to see colour, but they need brighter light.

Will it form a shadow?

Science facts
You can see clearly through some materials because light travels straight through them; they are called transparent materials. Other materials allow only some light to go through them; they are called translucent materials. Materials that allow no light to pass through them are called opaque materials. A shadow is formed when an opaque or translucent object blocks the light.

Science quiz
Use a black pencil or pen to draw in the shadows in this picture.

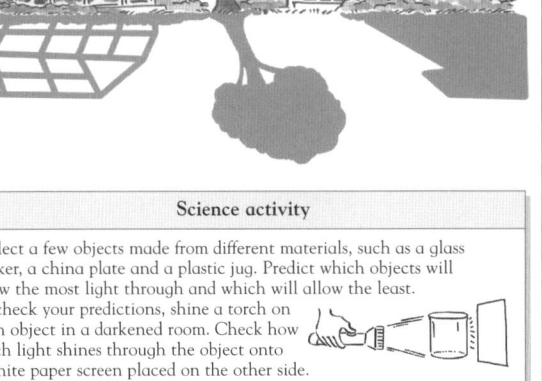

Science activity

Collect a few objects made from different materials, such as a glass beaker, a china plate and a plastic jug. Predict which objects will allow the most light through and which will allow the least. To check your predictions, shine a torch on each object in a darkened room. Check how much light shines through the object onto a white paper screen placed on the other side.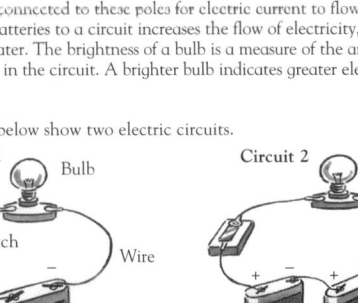

There should not be much of a shadow from the greenhouse, unless your child draws in the shadows of the metal struts. In the *Science activity*, however, your child will see that even transparent objects block a small amount of light from going through.

What affects the size of a shadow?

Science facts
Light travels in straight lines. It radiates out in all directions from a light source. When an object blocks the light, a shadow is formed. The shadow will get bigger if the light source is moved closer to the object. Moving the object farther away from its shadow will also make the shadow bigger.

Science quiz
John was making a shadow-puppet theatre. He used a sheet stretched between two table legs as his screen and a bright lamp as his light source. He made the shape of a person from cardboard and stuck it on a stick, but the shadow of the shape was too big for the screen.

How could he make the shadow smaller? List two ways.

John could make the shadow smaller either by moving the puppet

closer to the screen or by moving the lamp farther back.

Science activity

Find out how you can make a shadow bigger. Use a bottle or a book as your object, a torch as your light source and a wall as your screen. You will need a tape measure or a ruler to measure the size of the shadow. How big can you make the shadow? How small can you make it? How did you change the size of the shadow?

In the *Science activity*, encourage your child to first place the object in a fixed position and move the torch closer and farther away from it. Then ask him or her to move the object away from the wall, leaving the torch in a fixed position.

What do batteries do?

Science facts
Batteries are a source of electricity. They are made up of one or more 1.5-V units, called cells. (V stands for volt, which is a measure of how much energy a battery has.) A 3-V battery is made of two 1.5-V cells linked together. A battery has two ends called the positive (+) and negative (–) poles. Wires must be connected to these poles for electric current to flow in a circuit. Adding more batteries to a circuit increases the flow of electricity, making the current greater. The brightness of a bulb is a measure of the amount of electric current in the circuit. A brighter bulb indicates greater electric current.

Science quiz
The drawings below show two electric circuits.

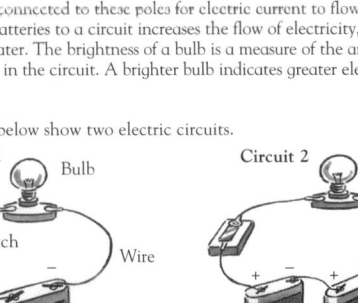

Circuit 1
Bulb
Switch
Wire
Battery

Circuit 2

What is the difference between these two circuits?
Circuit 1 has one battery, while circuit 2 has two batteries.

In which circuit is the bulb brighter when the switch is closed? Why?
The bulb is brighter in circuit 2 because there are two batteries and
so there is more electric current.

Science activity

Make a torch using a cardboard tube, a battery, some wires, a bulb and a switch. Add another battery, making sure that you connect one battery's positive pole to the other's negative pole. Add a third battery. When is the bulb the brightest?

For the *Science activity*, use a bulb suited to 3.5 V in order to get a range of brightness. Do not use more than three batteries as the bulb may break. Avoid using rechargeable batteries as they can heat up if incorrectly connected.

Do more bulbs mean more light? ⭐

Science facts
Inside a light bulb, there is a thin wire called a filament. When electricity flows through this filament, some of the electrical energy is changed into light energy. The flow of electricity, or the electric current, is slower when there is a bulb in a circuit. If another bulb is added, the current slows down even more and the filaments in each bulb do not glow as brightly.

Science quiz
Dipak made the circuit shown below. He was surprised that the bulbs were so dim that they were hardly glowing. He did not have another battery, so how do you think he could have changed the circuit to make the light brighter?

He could have made the lights brighter by removing one or two of the

bulbs and their bulb holders from the circuit.

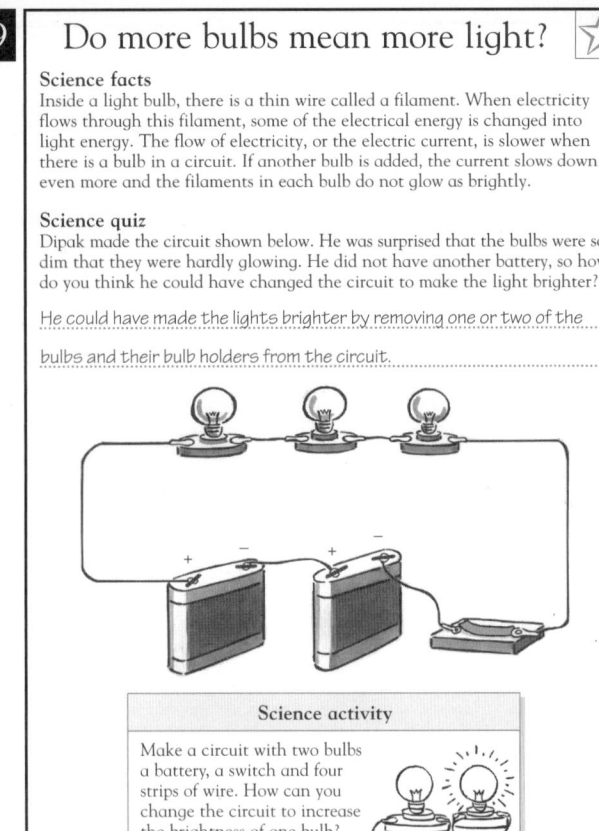

Science activity

Make a circuit with two bulbs a battery, a switch and four strips of wire. How can you change the circuit to increase the brightness of one bulb?

To make the bulb brighter in the activity, your child will have to take the other bulb and its holder out of the circuit. Taking just the bulb out of its holder and leaving the holder will make the circuit incomplete and the other bulb will not glow at all.

⭐ What does a circuit diagram show?

Science facts
Electricity always flows around a circuit in one direction – from the negative (–) pole of a battery to the positive (+) pole. This flow of electricity is called the electric current. Electrical circuits can be represented by special diagrams. There is a symbol for each electrical component in a circuit.

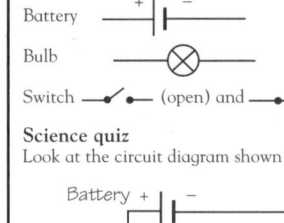 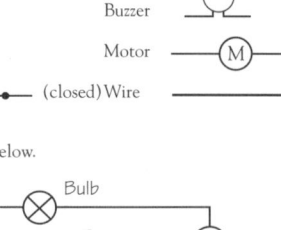

Battery   Buzzer

Bulb   Motor

Switch —/— (open) and —•— (closed) Wire ————

Science quiz
Look at the circuit diagram shown below.

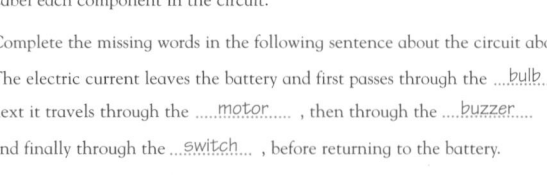

Label each component in the circuit.

Complete the missing words in the following sentence about the circuit above.

The electric current leaves the battery and first passes through the ...._bulb_.... ,

next it travels through the ...._motor_.... , then through the ...._buzzer_....

and finally through the ...._switch_.... , before returning to the battery.

Science activity

Draw some symbols of electrical components on different cards. Using lines to represent wires, arrange the cards to make a circuit. With your finger, trace the path of electricity around the circuit from one end of the battery to the other.

Help your child make models of different circuits by arranging the symbols in different orders. Ask him or her to name the components and trace the path of the current. Your child should always start at the negative pole and end at the positive pole.

Can you draw a circuit diagram? ⭐

Science facts
A simple circuit diagram is usually set out as a rectangle. It shows how the components, such as bulbs, switches, batteries and wires are linked in a circuit.

Science quiz
Look at these two pictures of circuits.

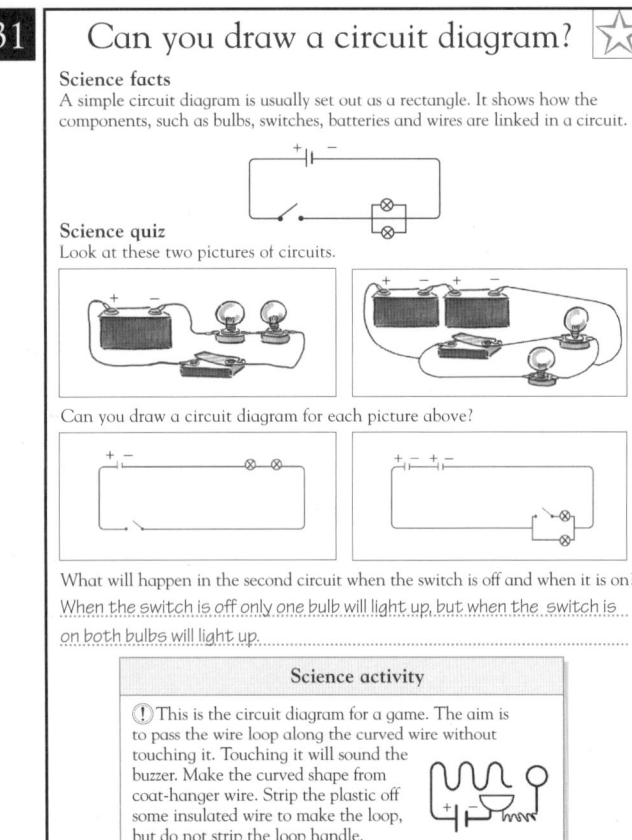

Can you draw a circuit diagram for each picture above?

What will happen in the second circuit when the switch is off and when it is on?
When the switch is off only one bulb will light up, but when the switch is
on both bulbs will light up.

Science activity

⚠ This is the circuit diagram for a game. The aim is to pass the wire loop along the curved wire without touching it. Touching it will sound the buzzer. Make the curved shape from coat-hanger wire. Strip the plastic off some insulated wire to make the loop, but do not strip the loop handle.

The two circuits in the _Science quiz_ show how bulbs can be connected in series or in parallel. Point out the difference to your child. The loop in the _Science activity_ acts like a switch. When it touches the wire, the circuit is completed and the buzzer goes off.

⭐ Will it switch on or off?

Science facts
Electricity will flow in a circuit only if there are no breaks in it. A switch is a useful device because you can use it to make a break in a circuit and stop the electricity flowing whenever you want. You use switches to turn electric lights and other household appliances on and off.

This is the symbol for an open switch. —/— This switch is off.
This is the symbol for a closed switch. —•— This switch is on.

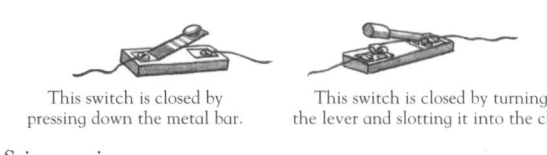

This switch is closed by pressing down the metal bar.

This switch is closed by turning the lever and slotting it into the clip.

Science quiz
Look at this circuit diagram.

What is the least number of switches you
need to close to make the bulb light up? _Two switches_

Which switches are they? _Switches 1 and 4_

Science activity

Make a pressure switch using two sheets of aluminium foil slightly separated by a few balls of cotton wool. Use this in a circuit with a battery and a buzzer to make a burglar alarm. When the two sheets touch each other, the switch closes and the circuit is completed. What happens when you step on your pressure switch?

Practise using different arrangements of cotton wool and foil to make the pressure switch in the _Science activity_. The circuit will be completed only when the two sheets of foil touch each other and the switch closes.